AN INSPIRING AND EMPOWERING FINANCIAL GUIDE FOR WOMEN OVER FORTY

ARWEN BECKER

SHE HANDLED IT!® RETIREMENT
An Inspiring and Empowering Financial Guide for Women Over Forty

Copyright © 2023 by Arwen Becker

All rights reserved. No part of this book may be used or reproduced in any manner whatsoever without prior written consent of the author, except as provided by the United States of America copyright law.

Published by LIFE with Arwen, Inc.

ISBN: 978-1-7353905-1-2

Cover Design: Yna
Cover Photo: Shutterstock
Back Photo: Fischer Wallace
Interior Layout: Mike Murray, pearhouse.com

> This book is designed to provide authoritative information on the subject of personal finances. It is sold with the understanding that the author is not engaged in rendering legal, accounting or other professional services by publishing this book. As each individual situation is unique, questions relevant to personal finances and specific to the individual should be addressed to an appropriate professional to ensure that the situation has been evaluated carefully and appropriately. The author disclaims any liability, loss, or risk which is incurred as a consequence directly or indirectly, of the use and application of any of the contents of this work. This book provides numerous charts and illustrations, they are intended for illustrative purposes only, and past performance does not guarantee future performance. While all of the stories and anecdotes described in this book are based on true experiences, most of the names are pseudonyms and some situations and characteristics have been changed slightly for educational purposes and to protect each individual's privacy.

Truly inspiring…this book will prepare any woman to believe that a great retirement is within her grasp!
> – DAVID BACH, 10X NYT BESTSELLING AUTHOR, INCLUDING *SMART WOMEN FINISH RICH*® AND *THE LATTE FACTOR*®

This book is anything but conventional, and I couldn't put it down! Arwen's candid and personal stories shed light on the fear and shame that many women feel about money. It provides practical tools and clear steps to help you move forward. You can definitely handle this!
> – AMBERLY LAGO, BESTSELLING AUTHOR OF *TRUE GRIT AND GRACE*, TEDX SPEAKER, AND *TRUE GRIT AND GRACE* PODCAST HOST

"Arwen, am I going to be broke?" These words echo the single greatest fear of most retirees. With captivating storytelling and simple clarity, Arwen leads us on the quest to protect ourselves as women approaching retirement. Arwen simplifies two things: the problem and the solution. The problem: women often run out of money as we age without real retirement planning, because we take care of everyone but ourselves. The solution: simple math and financial self-care. This book will make every woman feel empowered and focused. It does not matter who handles the finances in your home; what matters is that we women pay attention. This is not your father's investment book—this is a new woman's financial Bible. Brava, Arwen!
> – CATHY SIKORSKI, ESQ., NATIONAL SPEAKER, AND AUTHOR OF *WHO MOVED MY TEETH?* AND *12 CONVERSATIONS: HOW TO TALK TO ALMOST ANYONE ABOUT LONG-TERM CARE PLANNING*

When I started reading SHE HANDLED IT!® RETIREMENT *I simply could not put it down. While women are known for putting everyone else first, Arwen ripped open the curtain to show you what's really happening. She gives you the what, the why, and most importantly the how to position yourself as a woman armed with the education to be financially savvy and happy. It is the newest tool in my toolbox.*
> – JUDY HOBERMAN, IHEART RADIO AND PODCAST HOST OF *SELLING IN A SKIRT*, TEDX SPEAKER, AND BESTSELLING AUTHOR OF *WALKING ON THE GLASS FLOOR*

Arwen, you did it! When one has grown weary of stereotypical stories about women and money—then this book is the one you need. Most stories about women and their money are narrated like a scary dream: if you spend money, then watch out—you'll become a bag lady. If you save money, then guess what—you did not save enough money. In SHE HANDLED IT!®

RETIREMENT, Arwen shares true stories which include growing your money confidence, the importance of investment persistence, the critical need of longevity planning today, and ultimately relishing your work. Do yourself a favor: take a weekend, read the book, and start working on your money plan. Friends, you deserve this!

— SHERYL BROWN-HICKERSON, CEO OF FEMALES & FINANCE, NATIONAL SPEAKER, AND HOST OF *THE F WORD* PODCAST

With her refreshingly honest, focused, and passionate voice, Arwen unpacks why—because of different life experiences, aspirations, and needs around money—an empathetic, values-based, confident approach to retirement planning for women is needed. This book provides just that—a blueprint for a fresh, vibrant, new conversation.

— SARAH KING, CO-FOUNDER AND CEO OF OBU INVEST, TELEGRAPH AND NATWEST TOP 100 ENTREPRENEURS TO WATCH, AND UKBAA FINALIST - INVESTMENT IN DIVERSITY CHAMPION

There is no one that has *more passion* for helping women than Arwen. Her ability to connect with people, and her serving heart, has provided her with the opportunity to make an incredible impact all over the country. This book is an easy read, and the strategies are simple to implement. Arwen can take complex concepts and make them approachable to everyone. Enjoy this read; you will love it!

— MEGAN JONES, PRESIDENT JONES ADVISORY GROUP, HOST OF RADIO AND TV SHOW *MONEY MATTERS WITH MEGAN*

SHE HANDLED IT!® RETIREMENT is not just another finance guide—it's a beacon of hope and empowerment for midlife women. Arwen artfully weaves her transformational journey—from financial naivety to a recognized expert—with the poignant tales of women who sought guidance from her retirement firm. In an era where many women tread cautiously around the subject of investments, and where emotions like shame, doubt, and fear immobilize us, Arwen presents a transformative strategy. Guided by Arwen's genuine heart, deep wisdom, and touching vulnerability, readers will find not just financial advice, but a soulful companion lighting the path towards a prosperous tomorrow without compromising the joys of today.

— RAKEL CHAFIR, TEDX SPEAKER, BESTSELLING AUTHOR, AND HIGH-PERFORMANCE COACH

I've known Arwen for over a decade, and have seen up close her passion for helping women succeed with their finances. Arwen is changing how the financial industry serves women. This book inspires women to lean into the greatness ahead of them in the second half of their lives!

– CODY FOSTER, FOUNDER OF ADVISORS EXCEL, FORTUNE MAGAZINE'S TOP 100 BEST SMALL/MEDIUM WORKPLACES FOR MILLENNIALS AND IS CERTIFIED A GREAT PLACE TO WORK®

Arwen's commitment to level up women not only in their finances but in their life is truly admirable. This book will give you the confidence to know that you are not alone and that no matter where you are you can win in your finances and in life. This book gives you permission to want something bigger for yourself and all other women around you.

– EVA MACIAS, NATIONAL SPEAKER, CEO OF EVA MACIAS & ASSOCIATES, BESTSELLING AUTHOR OF *A LATINA'S GUIDE TO MONEY*

Some of the most important skills I teach when training businesspeople to lead talk shows are how to engage the listener with intriguing, accessible ideas, and to connect so intimately that it feels to the listener as if the radio host is speaking directly to them. With SHE HANDLED IT!® RETIREMENT, *Arwen accomplishes all of this without the advantage of the spoken word. You'll learn more in this captivating book than you would by studying finance textbooks, because Arwen slips into the chair next to you and illustrates concepts through stories, anecdotes, and real-life experiences. In this way, new understanding seeps into your soul and, in the end, it gushes forth in the form of confidence! Confidence that you—yes, YOU—can handle it too!*

– MICKEY O'NEILL, NATIONAL SPEAKER, AUTHOR OF *HOW TO DO TALK RADIO FOR FUN AND PROFIT*, CO-HOST OF RADIO SHOW *SUPERHEALTH* AND RADIO COACH

Having had the privilege to coach Arwen in her time at UW, I saw her deep desire to be her very best even while others weren't watching. Her drive for excellence, overcoming resistance and personal motivation inspired her teammates to develop their own greatness. She is proof that each challenge becomes a steppingstone for the next, contributing to personal growth and long-term success. Arwen understands the value of a great coach, a clear plan and willingness to execute. Zero question you will become a better version of yourself by reading this book!

- BILL GILLESPIE, ALL TIME WORLD RECORD BENCH PRESS HOLDER, 133 BENCH PRESS WORLD RECORDS, 30+ YEAR NFL/NCAA STRENGTH COACH

SHE HANDLED IT!® RETIREMENT is more than a collection of ideas and advice. It's a playbook for gaining freedom. If you dread financial resources out of fear or intimidation, you can rest assured, this book is different. Grounded in expertise and experience, Arwen's writing helped me gain insight into my life patterns and equipped me to start making informed, excited choices about my future financial security.

– DAPHNE J. VOUGHT, INTERNATIONAL SPEAKER, COACH, AND AUTHOR OF *WHAT'S YOUR SCARLET LETTER — RECOGNIZE YOUR HURTS, RELEASE YOUR SHAME, RECLAIM YOUR VOICE*

Arwen's passion to lead women is like none other. She loves deeply; she encourages, inspires, and challenges us women all to live life to its fullest. SHE HANDLED IT!® RETIREMENT is a must-read; Arwen will move your heart. She will inspire your life and teach you solid financial principles to empower you!

– STEPHANIE FULLERTON, NATIONAL SPEAKER, RADIO HOST OF FULLERTON FINANCIAL HOUR, AND AUTHOR OF *LIVING A HAPPY, HEALTHY, AND INSPIRED RETIREMENT*

Reading this book is like sitting down to share a bottle of wine with your best girlfriend. Arwen turns boring spreadsheets and cold numbers into funny, raw, and real stories that inspire and inform. By the time you're done, you'll have learned how to navigate the sometimes confusing, often intimidating, and mostly male-dominated world of finance like a pro. Every woman who has ever struggled to make sense of her finances needs to read this book!

– MARCELLA ALLISON, AUTHOR OF *WHY DIDN'T ANYBODY TELL ME THIS SH*T BEFORE: WIT AND WISDOM FROM WOMEN IN BUSINESS*

The brilliance of this book lies not just in Arwen's storytelling, but in her ability to shine a light on the underlying dynamics which drive women to make crucial money mistakes. She lays herself on the page, allowing women the permission to take their own inventory without the often-associated guilt and shame, and at the same time holds their feet to the fire to do something different. Then, she tells them exactly what to do. If you want a gentle, instructional, yet highly entertaining kick in the ass, this book is for you!

– ABBY HAVERMANN, OWNER OF ABBY HAVERMANN COACHING AND CONTRIBUTING AUTHOR OF *THE BEAUTY OF AUTHENTICITY*

It takes an incredibly bright, intelligent, passionate, and courageous person to take a stand for positive change. In this refreshing book, Arwen takes a strong stand for all women—and it came at a critical time. You won't just learn impressive but practical financial strategies, you'll develop mature core values and thought leadership which will seal your transformation. Win the New Game with Arwen's guide.

– AMBER VILHAUER, DIGITAL MARKETING SPECIALIST,
OWNER OF NGNG ENTERPRISES, INC.

I count the day I heard Arwen speak as one of the key turning points in my life. I went from being vaguely ashamed about my financial situation, to having a pathway to a plan! No jargon–just heart-filled passion to guide me towards an approach for the rest of my life. Arwen's passion for delivering actionable and smart financial know-how to women burns bright white. It is unstoppable. Her logical is irrefutable, and even the kicks on the shin are delivered with compassionate accuracy! Read this book and get bounced out of your complacency!

– ALAYNE REESBERG, CHIEF EXECUTIVE AT DESIGN FOR GOOD -
THE WORLD'S MOST AMBITIOUS AND IMPACTFUL DESIGN NON-PROFIT

Arwen is on a mission to empower women in a male-dominated industry. She has lived through, and genuinely understands, the financial pitfalls that women uniquely face. Arwen's perspective and authenticity are what make her new book so refreshing. **She Handled It!® Retirement** *will inspire you to take the action that will change the course of your life indefinitely!*

– WENDY POSILLICO, MINDSET COACH, SPEAKER,
AND FOUNDER OF STRANDS OF STRENGTH

Arwen's approach to finance and life is inspiring and insightful. I love the journey she shares to help other women understand the power we hold in our own lives.

– KERSTIN O'SHIELDS, NATION'S LEADING BODY LANGUAGE
STRATEGIST, NATIONAL SPEAKER, PERFORMING SOPRANO,
AND FOUNDER OF THE BODY LANGUAGE STRATEGY ACADEMY

I have known Arwen for over 15 years, she has always had this way of communicating practical ways of taking charge of your financial, physical, and emotional health, by simply exampling what it looks like, not just talking about it. This book takes powerful lived experience, tested and practiced habits, and makes it relevant to the real-life woman of today. She takes the phrase "living your best life" and shows you how attainable and achievable it really is. This book will be a game changer to whoever picks it up and decides they need and want something better!

– FAHREN JOHNSON, YOUTH AND COMMUNITY ADVOCATE, ARTIST, AUTHOR OF *A VIEW OF REDEMPTION*

In SHE HANDLED IT!® RETIREMENT, Arwen strips away the mysteries about money, personal finance and investing so that you feel empowered and inspired to take action today. Sharing best practices through her own relatable experiences guides you to understanding your next best financial step.

– DEBBIE PAGE, ENTREPRENEUR, BUSINESS COACH, AND LEADING AUTHORITY ON CASH FLOW AND PROFITABILITY FOR WOMEN BUSINESS OWNERS

DEDICATION

This book is dedicated to the thousands of women I have met over the years who have handled it. Those who have found a way to overcome major challenges in life and do it with grace. Women who are leaning thoughtfully into the second half of their life, taking personal responsibility, and doing it with gusto!

To the mothers and grandmothers determined to live a financially secure life and pass along their wisdom to truly impact the next generation.

This is also dedicated to all the women I've yet to meet, who have wondered, Is it too late for me? or Will I be okay? For all those that have felt dismissed or talked over in the area of money. To women who have ever felt a twinge of embarrassment that they don't understand this money thing or who wonder if they ever will.

Your anxiety and embarrassment end here. Confidence will abound. I promise to leave you better than I found you!

#shehandledit

TABLE OF CONTENTS

INTRODUCTION	1
WHY WOMEN	25
VALUES-BASED PLANNING	37
GOOD NEWS	61
NOT SO GOOD NEWS	73
YOU NEED A PLAN	87
INCOME FOR LIFE	103
MARKET RISK & FEES	133
TAXES & REQUIRED MINIMUM DISTRIBUTIONS	153
LONGEVITY & HEALTHCARE	165
PROTECTION FOR THE UNEXPECTED	181
WHY HIRE AN ADVISOR?	191
GETTING STARTED & ORGANIZED	213
CONCLUSION	225
RESOURCES: BECOMING A BETTER HUMAN	229
ABOUT THE AUTHOR	233
SPECIAL THANKS	235

CHAPTER 1

INTRODUCTION

> *You're a fighter. You're stronger than you know. Just don't give up.*

SHE HANDLED IT

"Your mom doesn't have a credit card? How is that possible?"

It's funny, the things that stay with us from childhood. At that age, we're young and have no control over the way things are—but we absorb everything. Fundamentally, we just want to be loved by our families and peers. Myself, I remember feeling so small when the popular seventh-grade girl—complete with designer clothes and expensive shoes—smirked after telling me that we should go shopping together at the mall. She was pointing out the fact that I had arrived on my first day of seventh grade in handmade clothes. Everyone else had store-bought outfits and brand names, but I was different. Foreclosure had forced our family to move from my childhood home into a rental, and times were extremely tough. I didn't have clothes from the mall nor the money to purchase nice things.

Neither my father nor my stepdad could provide for us financially. My mom did what most mothers do: *she handled it*. She handled it by working a job she despised as a lunch lady at the rival junior high school. But her job had the benefits of health insurance, and she had the same days off as my sister and me. Mom handmade our clothes, which was a true labor of love—but that kind of love wasn't considered fashionable in those days. Handmade was perfectly fine for biscuits, greeting cards, and Christmas ornaments, but for seventh grade girls, home-stitched clothes weren't going to get you places. We humans put a lot of emphasis on conformity—and appearances—especially in those formative teen years. My sister and I understood that we wore different clothes because we *were* different.

Hold on for a second here—please don't misunderstand me. As a woman with more than half her life behind her, I am so grateful for what I did have and the things that my parents and community provided. All things considered; I have had a very blessed life. Growing up, I was fortunate to have a roof over my head, food on the table, people who loved me, and a safe place to attend school and play sports. Goodness knows that many children don't have those kinds of assurances. But at that moment in time, I was an immature and self-consumed junior high kid, comparing myself to what I saw around me. In my formative years, I didn't have the wisdom and appreciation that I would later have. Today, decades later, I truly understand the privileges I had even as I struggled to fit in financially with my peers. As a young girl growing up, I felt constantly reminded of what I *didn't have* instead of seeing my many blessings.

AMAZING SEAMSTRESS

One of those blessings was that my mom was—and is—an amazing seamstress. I remember walking through the aisles of fabric stores with her and helping decide what cool fabric she would use to make my next outfit. I would beg her to purchase materials that were more expensive, and I often caused considerably more work for her with my hopeful teenage pattern choices.

These memories are etched into my mind: glaring fluorescent lights shining on the rolls of fabric, and the old women who worked there (in fairness, everyone is old when you're twelve). Above all, I remember the walls of taupe file cabinets jam-packed with patterns. If there was an event, or a school dance, I would flip through the pattern books searching for that one perfect dress my mother would make for me. Sitting at the tables, I would thumb through the catalogues, admire the carefree models, and pray that my mom would be able to produce that one special dress that would make the boys look, and make me feel special.

She could. *She always could.*

I had every color and pattern of spandex known to man during that time (ah, the 1980s). And alterations, geez, she worked pure magic! Her skills were in high demand during the late eighties, when we wanted our jeans skintight (so much so that we needed someone else to help pull them off at the end of the day). If those jeans ever got wet, so help you, you'd be stuck wearing them for hours! Mom never had to say "no" for difficulty, but often had to hesitate because of the price to buy the pattern and the fabric to go along with it. Tragically, sewing is not a hereditary skill. I can't even mend a hem.

Deep down, I relished the fact that she hand-crafted stunning dresses with luscious fabrics—they were tailored to fit like a glove, and I knew I'd never run into an embarrassing "who wore it best" situation. She made all four of my homecoming dresses, my junior prom dress, and my wedding dress! The original pattern for my wedding dress was traditional and plain, so Mom dazzled it up by hand-sewing hundreds of crystals and fabric flowers, most of which went on the train that I wore for only thirty minutes or so during the ceremony. After thirty-some hours enhancing that dress, Mom said she would never do it again, no matter how much someone might pay!

That kind of work demonstrates the true love of a mother, the gift of a mom.

Thank you, Mom.

I JUST WANTED TO FIT IN

Thinking back to middle school, as much as I admired my mom and her handy-dandy skills, I was still embarrassed when other girls would talk to me about my clothes. They'd give me a compliment, then follow with a question, such as, "Where did you buy it?" And even though my apparel was personalized, expertly made, and perfectly fit, I ached desperately to go to the mall and pick out an outfit like all my friends. I longed to have a neon t-shirt that declared G-U-E-S-S in huge letters right across the front. That would prove that we had money to casually spend on frivolous, pricey t-shirts bought while *shopping*. To this day, I avoid the mall like the plague, because my negative memories are so ingrained. For me, it will forever feel like a place I do not belong.

At a very early age, I understood that life was not fair. There were *haves and have-nots*, and there was a lot to worry about. Shame, powerlessness, and resentment began to build deep within me. I wanted so much out of life, but I was afraid that something would always be in the way.

I felt anxiety as a young girl, and into my teens, I felt a constant need to belong. The normal insecurities felt by any young woman at that age were compounded by my desire to really make it and prove myself. I had talents and skills, and I threw my energy into activities to create an identity. But was I content? Honestly, I was trying to fill the void of a dysfunctional family.

The lack of relationship with my nomadic biological father and a dishonest, alcoholic stepdad left me feeling that I had to figure things out by myself. And watching my mother try to over-compensate for the difficult situation both men put her in was very stressful. My athletic and academic achievements gave me a sense of worth, and the praise from many other father figures, but it came later in life—at a cost. Above all, I didn't want to be known as the girl *without*. I just wanted to feel loved, cherished, and special. My little girl's heart cried out to have a dad that showed love and provided me feelings of safety and security. At the same time, I longed to see my stepdad care for and support my mother in big ways and small. Neither happened. My mom had to do it all and more, and that made me deeply angry towards both my dads.

MONEY WAS ALWAYS AN ISSUE

Throughout much of my youth, there were barrage of reminders about my family's financial situation. I felt the weight of the financial stress, and observed closely all the ways it affected my mom. She didn't have the tools or the knowledge to dig us all out of the hole; her plan was to keep going, hold her breath, and just work harder. I begrudged the phone calls that came in during dinnertime (in the era before caller ID). I would jump from the table to answer, thinking it might be one of my friends. Instead, I would hear the stern voice of a man on the other end, demanding, "May I speak to your mother?" I would hold the phone out to her, while she whispered while waving her hands desperately: "I'm not here! Tell him I'm not here!" Invariably, the person on the phone was another bill collector. These intrusive calls and power shut-off notices were all too familiar.

No matter how hard my mom worked, we had serious challenges at home. My father rarely paid child support and my stepdad consistently made terrible financial choices (some minor, some very major); because of his alcoholism, my mom was always left picking up the pieces. We didn't take family vacations, try out new restaurants, or ski in the local mountains—nor did we own our house. And there was the blue rattling Datsun that picked us up from school to take us to Value Village to purchase secondhand goods. We lived in a rental that never felt like the kind of dwelling I could comfortably invite friends to. Most of all, it was the instability that ran our lives—that's what really hurt. There was always something telling us "no" and "that's for everyone else, but not for you." As a kid, those kinds of messages stay with you forever.

I felt like an outsider and a failure, as if I had done something wrong. Shame mounted.

With no reliable father figure, no financial security, and no spiritual guidance, I sought to fill the void with sports and school—trying any way possible to receive an "atta girl!" via MVP awards or stellar report cards. Without proper examples or resources, I made my way by sheer effort and determination.

THE RIGHT COACH AT THE RIGHT TIME

The classroom and athletic field were two areas where I could control my situation and receive positive feedback. These successes made me feel good, if only for a moment. One thing I believe deeply in is mentorship, and I was blessed to have a few tremendous mentors in my earlier years who helped guide me during vulnerable times. One of these individuals was my first volleyball coach, Colleen Aldrich. She had the ability to motivate and teach an entire team of junior high girls in a way that opened our eyes to greater lessons. Leading with love and compassion, she left such a giant impact on me. Looking back, I realize that she was instructing us out of love, rather than competition or power, and having a positive relationship with her made me feel good about who I was and what I was doing. In those three years under her direction, I fell in love with the sport of volleyball, and Coach Aldrich was a meaningful role model during a time when I was starting to really look at the world around me, and more importantly, my place in it.

Most of all, Coach Aldrich helped develop within me certain qualities that cannot be bought with cash—she inspired strength and perseverance, but also integrity and kindness. Only experience can bring those out in a person. Finally, I was succeeding at something that didn't come with a price tag…hard work was something I could afford!

SHEER DETERMINATION OVER NATURAL TALENT

I wasn't class valedictorian—I failed my first SAT exam (whoops)—but I worked hard and graduated with honors and a 3.9 GPA. Many of the other girls were more naturally gifted athletes than I was, but relentless practice can get you quite far, and I was voted most athletic in a 4-A school of 1,500 students. I set records in swimming, went to state twice in softball and once in track, and was named volleyball MVP in the state of Washington my senior year. Girls who had more talent couldn't keep up with my tenacity—I drilled nights, weekends, and mornings for that recognition, to feel valuable and important. I wanted deeply to feel loved and valued.

Unfortunately, affirmations don't pay the bills. My hyper-planning brain worked overtime to find a way out of a life that was always monetarily lacking. I babysat twenty-three out of thirty days a month each summer, but it wasn't enough to resolve my aching insecurity.

Through a relentless pursuit, I learned a lot of things the hard way. I struggled on my own to learn the healthy kinds of coping skills that would bridge the gap between a painful situation (feeling stuck) and the freedom to go where I really wanted to be. Life is hard enough, and we do the best we can with what we have, but my early life financial situation always made me feel I had done something wrong. We as women need to be able to ask for help (most of us struggle to do so), and quit trying to control situations that are beyond our control. This was a skill I would not learn until many decades later.

SOLID PLANS START WITH BLUEPRINTS—OR IS THAT BLUE EYES?

By the time I entered high school, I had created the perfect plan for my life. I was not going to have to struggle with money, ever. My brilliant fifteen-year-old idea was to find a nice boy with a financially savvy disposition and marry him. Foolproof.

I was a sophomore in high school when my friends introduced me to a tall young man with bright blue eyes. Success was written all over him and it was imprinted into his DNA. He was a born salesman, forged in a family of entrepreneurs, and when I looked at him, I saw my financially secure future. I fell in love with a fairytale image, a beautiful vision of us together, and a life of financial stability. We dated through high school, and as graduation neared, I received full-ride scholarship offers to play volleyball at the University of South Florida and Colorado State University. Meanwhile, he signed on to play baseball with the University of Washington.

Dilemma.

With the full wisdom of my seventeen years, I declared, "I'm going to the University of Washington!" and listened as the air was sucked out of the room by the collective gasps of my mother and select volleyball coaches. They gently (and not-so-gently) presented the drawbacks to my plan: I was forfeiting two full-ride scholarship offers, pinning major life decisions on a high school boyfriend, and making short-sighted and immature choices.

But I was determined to prove them wrong (insert overwhelming stubbornness and pride here).

College was an incredibly important time for me. For one, it was the first time in my life that I wasn't the athletic top dog. Being the second shortest of eighteen girls, I wasn't able to just get by on raw talent; I had to put in serious commitment and focus on being prepared. Sports have always been a huge part of my life, so this was a humbling time where I had to dedicate everything I had to get the success I desired. This took a lot of self-motivation. I had to learn how to move faster, jump higher, increase my endurance (taller athletes don't get shorter as they get tired) and lift more weight.

I can tell you that in my years as a financial advisor, that application is one of life's most important lessons. You can't just want financial security and have it work out. It takes effort, consistency, and a plan to reach your goals. Even more, it means getting help from those who know more that you do.

SUCCESS COMES FROM DISCIPLINE

I was truly blessed to meet one of the best humans on the planet during my time at the UW who taught me these life-lessons in my late teens, exactly when I was looking for a father figure to believe in me. This was the head weight-lifting coach, Bill Gillespie. Bill had a soft-spoken voice and a gentle demeanor, but he refused to let anyone shirk their responsibilities. From him, I learned not only the value of teamwork, but the willingness to work a little bit harder at every turn. Show up early, work out on holidays, set daily goals, and do your personal best—especially when no one is looking. Much of our success in life comes from discipline (not motivation, which is fickle). He taught me how to be dedicated on a personal and private level, and with everything I do.

Another thing I learned from Coach Gillespie is perseverance and long suffering: hard work never ends, and you never fully arrive. It truly is the journey you need to fall in love with, not the destination. In the most optimistic way, we are never going to be *done*. When I was personally seeing financial clients and creating retirement plans, I always reminded them that we were focused on creating the best future possible, but that we also needed to live our *best life* now. Albert Einstein famously said, *"Learn from yesterday, live for today, hope for tomorrow."* And do so responsibly! There will never come a time when all the life boxes have truly been checked, and that's a good thing. Life means growth.

I've rekindled my relationship with Coach Gillespie in the past few years, and he never ceases to amaze me. At the age of 62, he set the world record for the bench press. Keep in mind that he set that world record for all age brackets! In 2021 he benched 1,129.8 pounds! One thousand one hundred forty-two pounds! Knowing his work ethic and determination, this success comes as no surprise. He was working on that goal when I knew him in his thirties, and it is thrilling to know that he achieved it thirty years later. But as a man with a deep passion for athletes, he's already back to work helping more young, impressionable, and struggling athletes move past their mental limitation and soar. His guidance helps others in all areas of life, not only in the gym.

Looking back now, I see that my greatest mentors were people I was drawn to because they were enormously positive and loving. These were qualities I was desperately searching for in my relationships, and their attention made me feel alive.

PROVED THEM WRONG

I went on to graduate from college and was the first at everything in my peer group. First to get married. First to buy a brand-new car. First to buy a house.

My new husband was as instantly successful as I had imagined he would be, and there was no more crappy Plymouth Horizon in my life; we bought a brand-new royal blue Lexus G300 off the showroom floor. As a child, I had only taken one vacation my family: a week on the coast of Oregon. Now, I was hopping on planes to Puerto Rico, Mexico, Maui, the Virgin Islands, New York, and so on. We were the youngest members of a prestigious private country club—and I didn't even know how to golf!

My always hyper-vigilant young brain relaxed just the tiniest bit. My plan was working; rich husband, lovely house, fab car, and the job of my dreams. I proved them all wrong; my plan had actually worked!

LIONS, AND TIGERS, AND BEARS, *OH MY!*

From the tender age of five, it was my sole desire to work with animals. The question was *doing what?* Veterinarian work involved a lot of schooling and a confined office. Dolphin training seemed inhumane. Marine mammologist, perhaps. I wanted to be part of a greater mission that allowed me to work directly with many types of animals. Then I found it: wildlife rehabilitation.

When I graduated from UW with a B.S. in Zoology, I became the Assistant Clinic Director of the non-profit Sarvey Wildlife Care Center in Arlington, Washington. Mine was one of only two paid roles, overseeing 110 volunteers who, like me, were passionate about caring for sick, injured, and orphaned animals. I supervised more than 200 animals every day, performing a multitude of tasks. I might be cleaning wounds, assisting veterinarians with surgery, or suturing, stapling, and tube-feeding birds, mammals, and reptiles from across the state. On top of that, I trained volunteers, dealt with media, ran marketing campaigns, organized fundraising, scheduled educational events, and answered to the board of directors.

I cared for every kind of wild animal you could find in the state of Washington. Elephant seals, pelicans, bats, flying squirrels, grebes, loons, herons, turtles, snakes, beavers, falcons, butterflies (yes, people would bring us injured butterflies), hummingbirds, jays, black bears... the list goes on. I even assisted in a blood transfusion between two bald eagles, owned an *unreleasable* Eastern Gray squirrel, and was attacked by a 110-pound cougar (that story is in Chapter Eleven). Imagine bottle-feeding river otters, bobcats, deer, skunks, porcupines, harbor seals, and raccoons—it was awesome!

This was my first glimpse into living a rich life. Not a *moneyed life*, but a life full of wonder, passion, and devotion. I had a mission to help the helpless.

Each day began at the crack of dawn, and I jumped out of bed to drive forty-two miles and give all I had for ten + hours a day. It was not about money—I was following my calling and giving to something I believed in. It was very fulfilling to have such purposeful work, and to be part of such an incredible organization. The operation included more than a hundred people every week who sacrificed their time to volunteer and serve. I felt accomplished, fascinated, and captivated. It was the greatest job!

Things were great on the outside, and I was checking all the proverbial boxes on my *fix my life to-do list*. Find a driven young man? Check. Get married? Check. Buy a home? Check. Start a dream job? Check. Travel the world? Check. Money in the bank? Check. Bills paid? Check.

Happily ever after?

As the new millennium approached, the clinic director, the raptor specialist, and I drafted our thoughts for the board of directors, outlining how we might nourish this twenty-five-year-old non-profit into the future. The founder, battling cancer, was in failing health, and we feared the center would struggle if we didn't have a plan for succession when she passed. We spent each waking moment living and breathing animal rescue, and were sure the board would love our proposal, our dedication, and our forward thinking.

Turns out our plan was not the success we assumed it would be.

NEVER THE SAME

Little did I know, a single blinking light on my voicemail recorder would forever alter the trajectory of my twenty-four-year-old life.

"Arwen, this is Gary. I have been hired as an outside attorney to inform you that you have been fired from the Wildlife Center. Let me remind you this is private property, and if you step foot back on the property, we will call the police. Thank you for understanding and your cooperation in this matter. Goodbye."

Devastation. Despair. Confusion.

The day before, my co-workers and I had overseen two dozen volunteers and had been responsible for the 300 animals in our care. In one moment, all our hard work was deleted. It was the only job I have ever been fired from, and the only thing I ever wanted to do. It wasn't merely a job—it was my singular passion, everything that made getting out of bed worthwhile for me. One single message arrived to tell me that I was no longer necessary.

What the heck, God?

The founder had seen our proposal as a power play—an attempted coup. It was an excruciatingly painful experience, knowing that people I admired were assuming the worst of me. It was a hard business lesson, being misunderstood by an organization we cared so deeply about. Four years later, when the founder died and the center wobbled and suffered without a succession plan, it was agonizing to watch. I am proud to say, however, that Sarvey has managed to survive, and today continues the work I found so fulfilling.

DOWNWARD SPIRAL

Having been extricated from my dream career, I became a stay-at-home wife. I filled my time attempting new dinner recipes, going to the gym, and struggling to find something that made me feel worthwhile. Life became a lukewarm *Groundhog Day* of waking up and going through the motions: wash, rinse, and repeat. We had money, but it couldn't give me a sense of purpose or happiness.

I continued my trend of firsts: *first to get divorced.*

PAIN WITH A PURPOSE

Divorce was an agonizing way to realize that I had never paid my own bills. I had worked so hard on *our* life that I didn't even have friends of my own. Until then, everything had been focused on building an ideal married lifestyle that I hadn't given any thought to my own identity.

The priorities (my checklists) that I had rooted myself in were no longer relevant, and I felt an expansive void. What was wrong with me? Why couldn't I just be happy? As women, we are largely expected to follow certain social standards, and that is *good enough*. But what if those expectations don't work out? It was enough to be going through the stress of a divorce, as well as the added pressure of feeling I had done something wrong.

This kind of complex affects women in various stages of life, and often prevents them from seeking the appropriate help they need. If they don't fit the traditional definition of spouse, job, and kids, they may not feel confident asking for assistance and guidance. There are, for example, scores of financial advisors talking to couples for retirement planning. But how many advisors specialize in retirement planning for widows, singles, and divorcees?

As I was drawing off the money I was awarded in the divorce, I had extensive alone time in my strange new apartment. Those hours of silence drew out periods of intense, harrowing soul searching. No one can prepare you for that kind of life transition. Everything was uncertain. I didn't know what to do, or who I could depend on. But I couldn't run away or hide—it was all happening right there, in my heart and in my mind.

I had been so busy for so long—and now it all came to a screeching halt. For the first time in my life, I was without distractions: it was me and reality. What was I going to do with my life? Who was I going to be? Who did I *want* to be?

PERSONAL DEVELOPMENT

A friend introduced me to Amway—a network-based marketing company that specializes in consumables such as home, health, and beauty products (makeup, vitamins, paper towels, etc.). *The compa*ny pushed all members of the network in personal development, requiring a commitment to individual growth to draw other distributors into the company to collaborate.

I began to consume books such as *The 7 Habits of Highly Effective People, The 5 Love Languages, Confidence and Power in Dealing with People, Don't Sweat the Small Stuff, How to Win Friends and Influence People,* and *Being Happy,* to name a few. I began to experience the beauty of reading books on personal development. These books were like personal therapists that allowed me to *save face* in the areas I was falling short in, and I was able to glean wisdom that prevented me from making further personal mistakes. This was the start of my life-long pursuit to better myself in the most organic way (one that didn't cost me $130 an hour for an actual therapist)! It was a *choose your own adventure* as I could mature and study any topic I was struggling with. The value of doing internal work and reflection was one of the greatest lessons I learned during those painfully quiet times.

You've most likely been through something very similar, in your own life. The disappointment, frustration, loneliness, anxiety, self-doubt, and sorrow—you know exactly how it feels. You know how hard it is to start over again and wonder, "how am I going to do this?" But this is a book about resilience and self-education, so we don't stay in that pity place for long. We get honest, we set goals, we ask for help, we get up in the morning, and we handle it.

STOP WITH THE GOD TALK

It was then I began the journey back to myself. It required me to say *YES!* to new experiences, studying, growing, and trying unfamiliar things. Of course, it was terrifying and exhilarating to leave my comfort zone, but I was intrigued. One tiny source of irritation, however, was that many of the people focused on personal growth and change persistently mentioned God, and I found it very bothersome. This needed to stop. Like, yesterday.

The culture of Amway embraced and encouraged a Higher Power, and this was a serious drawback for me. Events opened with prayers, and the program regularly incorporated Sunday morning church services. I felt a serious conflict, because I wanted to do business and learn about myself, but I did not want to talk about God. Yet, I was making new friends and I enjoyed being with these people. They had lives and marriages I admired, they were fun, and they laughed a lot! Moreover, they radiated a kind of peace and joy for life that I desired for myself, and needed and wanted so deeply. I ached to belong, and I wanted nothing more than to feel meaning and purpose.

This community had a strong foundation, and I wanted to share in that security. They were happy even when things didn't go right, and they asked deeper questions. They didn't have to be multi-millionaires to live full and balanced lives, and I was attracted to that kind of philosophy. I was willing to do whatever it might take to feel good again, and this allowed me to open myself to all kinds of opportunities in order to gain the peace that they enjoyed.

One of my new Amway friends challenged me to begin studying books about spirituality, and invited me to church. I finally permitted myself to listen and take it all in, and started to realize that God truly did love me and had designed me with a purpose. My defenses began to soften. Slowly, I found myself letting go of some of my pain, and, instead, putting my faith in Him. I felt renewed as I was filled with His unconditional love. At last, the 24-year-old divorcée came to life with light, dignity, purpose, and vitality.

Jesus flooded into my life in April of 2000, washing into the holes of my existence. I had a sense of completion like nothing I had ever experienced, but with this realization came a different kind of weight.

I felt released from the burden of shame and shadows, but I could not move forward as the same person. I had a lot of changing to do. With renewed spirit, I was ready to make those changes.

SPIRITUAL GROWTH, DWINDLING BANK ACCOUNT

Being involved with Amway in the early 2000s helped me to network and develop, but I wasn't making money. And, while I was embracing the meaningful readings about emotions, empowerment, and joyful living, I wasn't reading the practical books about saving, investing, and developing financial skills. Books on the recommended reading list included *Rich Dad Poor Dad*, *Richest Man in Babylon*, *Think and Grow Rich*, and a new one to the list, *Smart Women Finish Rich*. But at the time, I avoided those financial lesson books, because they were about 401(k)s, IRAs, mutual funds, and other financial jargon, a.k.a. boring men's stuff. I still had the notion that someone else would take care of *that*.

Ironically, I later became the #1 teacher in the nation of *Smart Women, Smart Retirement*™, based on David Bach's book, *Smart Women Finish Rich*. David Bach himself took me under his wing, and mentored me personally, as I educated and inspired thousands of women through his *Smart Women Smart Retirement*™ seminar. Don't tell me God doesn't have a sense of humor!

Looking back, I wish I had been more responsible about educating myself in those vital areas so many years ago, but things are always clearer in retrospect. One might assume that divorce would have opened my eyes to the need for financial education, and that I would have seen the importance of being self-sufficient—but I wasn't there yet. There was still a lot of life learning just ahead of me.

PASSION SET ASIDE, TIME TO GET A *REAL* JOB

As I said before, I had never paid my own bills. I knew my first goal had to be finding a job that would pay enough money to cover my actual expenses. It was both an empowering and terrifying thought.

Many of the women I have worked with as an advisor came to me in similar situations. Maybe they were fresh from a divorce, newly widowed, or had to go to work in middle age: these are not circumstances we think about in the *American Dream*. But they are a reality. We aren't taught to organize ourselves for a "Plan B," and it can be devastating to feel that you must pick up the pieces and start from square one after years of doing something completely different. Moreover, if you've always depended on a spouse to make decisions or bring paychecks, it's hard to ask, "Now what?!"

A friend in mortgage services reached out to me with what she thought was a possible job lead. I was getting ready to start with a local temp agency, but she had bumped into a man at a Bellevue, Washington coffee shop who worked in financial services. He was just starting his own firm after years of experience with a national firm, and they exchanged business cards. As she began to leave, he quickly mentioned, "By the way, I'm looking for some help. If you know of anyone looking for a job, let me know."

She gave me his information, and after one job interview, I was hired.

Thus, I landed my first "real" job. That term makes me wince, because many people saw my role of running a non-profit not as "real" due to the minimal stipend I received. I consider the many stay-at-home moms who do not bring home a regular paycheck. Is that not a real job? What about daughters that care for ailing parents, is that less valuable than a man working construction or fresh college graduate training as an accountant? Any work you do that contributes to the well-being of those you love and influence is valuable. After all, where are our priorities? Money does not equate to being productive when we are talking about service and resources.

My new boss and I got along very well. I never would have dreamed, with my zoology degree, that I would take a position in the financial industry. Now, in many ways, finance can be uptight, stuffy, and extremely boring, but the advisor I was working for had the ability to make a conservative atmosphere fun and interesting. He was a big-picture thinker, and my focused planner-brain was just the opposite. It was a tremendous fit, though. He sketched broad ideas, and I would follow up with bulleted action points to bring his plans to fruition. He was the visionary, and I was strategist.

Weirdly, the work scratched an itch I had for math and puzzles—for turning a problem over and over until I found a solution. And I brought energy and dedication to this new role. My boss became an important mentor, and my eventual business partner.

Well, my business partner and my life partner…

THE ULTIMATE PARTNERSHIP

A few short years after accepting the position at the financial firm, I walked down the aisle to join Randy Becker (my boss) as his wife, cementing our total partnership. It was the best day of my life! Not only were we building our practice, but we built our family as we became the parents to three amazing boys—Morgan, Ashton, and Easton.

A single encounter at a downtown Bellevue coffee shop created beauty from my ashes. God has a habit of doing that.

> *"For I know the plans I have for you, declares the Lord, plans to prosper you and not to harm you, plans to give you a hope and a future."*
> *– JEREMIAH 29:11 NIV*

Yet, this isn't, "and then they lived Happily Ever After." *Remember, a man is not a financial plan.* Marrying a financial advisor, I would learn, is not a substitute for standing tall on your own two feet. I was still in my late twenties and beginning a new verse of the same song.

If you'd like to skip to something that reads closer to happily ever after, go to Chapter Three, because it gets worse before it gets better.

Working as a financial advisor, I have seen, firsthand, how the financial services industry speaks a very masculine language. Only about a quarter of financial advisors are women, and senior roles skew roughly eighty-five percent male. There are, however, many attentive male advisors across this nation who enjoy working with women and give them the respect they deserve. Randy is one of these individuals (as are many of the male advisors I currently mentor or have in the past). My husband is a wonder to watch in action. I have always felt such pride observing him with clients; watching Randy care for women and their families inspired me to want to be a part of this profession for the long term. He has a big heart and a bigger purpose. For him, it isn't just business, it's very much personal.

Seeing the impact he made motivated me to become a financial advisor, as well.

From his example, I saw firsthand that a woman doesn't necessarily need another female to advise her financially; she needs an advisor with the right qualities, regardless of gender, who will listen, commit time to educating her, thoughtfully understand her, be engaged, openly communicate with her, and who will work in her best interest.

REHABBING INJURED ANIMALS TO INSPIRING WOMEN— NOT THAT DIFFERENT

I went from resuscitating broken animals, or critters that were even just slightly off course, to doing something very similar for women in my own community. As I gained perspective from watching Randy work, I began to realize quite a few things about women-focused planning on my own. We women are natural planners and doers, and we value security. Taking charge of finances also means taking charge of our personal security, dreams, and goals.

Women are often caretakers and will sacrifice their own needs to help others. We will do everything possible to answer other people's cries for help, but we feel completely unable to ask for assistance when we, ourselves, most need it. Our culture teaches women to serve and give, and to never seek attention. Service is beautiful, but not when it means ignoring your own well-being! It's like traveling on an airplane, as the in-flight safety instructions tell us: *in the case of a change in cabin pressure, be sure to place the oxygen mask over your own face first before assisting anyone else, even your own children.* It does little good to save others when you don't even have your own basic plan in place.

Putting yourself first simply means not neglecting your own needs. When we, as women, take care of our own emotional, financial, and physical issues, we are then ready to give our best to others. We are taught to negate our needs, but that's a direct path to frustration and exhaustion. We can be loving and generous without being martyrs.

I am highly aware of the cultural, generational, and societal standards that hold us back, but this book isn't about injustice and weeping. It's about empowerment and triumph, to remind us all that it's time to step out of the shadows and live our full worth. Empowerment is a choice, and I'm excited to hold up the mirror that reflects your true value and potential. Instead of seeing finance as a stressful weakness—a constant problem—I want you to know that it is a key to your power.

> "The most common way people give up their power is by thinking they don't have any." – ALICE WALKER

PREPARE TO PREPARE

Now, this book is not intended to break down every financial tool and cover the ins and outs of industry terminology for pre- and post-retirees: that will come in due time. Also let me say that retirement discussion and planning is not just for those sixty and above; it is for those of you in your late forties and fifties—those that have more working years behind them than in front of them. Instead, my goal is to help you *prepare to prepare,* so it's okay if the mention of money still gives you worry, confusion, or discomfort. We'll get there. One of my best friends, Fahren, works with at-risk youth, and she frequently reminds me: *a student who doesn't have their basic needs met (food, safety, shelter, clothing) will not be able to perform optimally at school.* Thus, our goal here is to remove the fundamental, most obvious, obstacles that might prevent you from knowing what you need to know and being able to access the resources and answers that you require. Challenges to our basic needs can keep us stuck and miserable.

Getting your needs met will also build self-confidence, which leads to better decision-making!

Most importantly, please know that you are *not alone.* It may feel insurmountable to confront such big topics and terms, but you will have me here as your guide and cheer squad, taking you step by step.

Retirement planning is one of the most intimidating subjects when it comes to finance. You may be nearing the retirement planning phase (late forties and beyond), or are already a few years in, yet you do not know how to start or carry on the planning conversation. Let me remind you that this is *your life* and *your retirement,* so who else is going to make those decisions?

*You need basic no*urishment with *financial food* before you are ready to open your mind to the more complex concepts you will eventually need on your journey. Rest easy that this book is not filled with extensive financial gobbledygook—nor is it geared towards highly sophisticated investors. This is for those of us who sit on the edge during meetings with investment advisors or insurance people, nodding our heads and not wanting to say anything for fear of being judged. We don't want to look stupid. We don't know what to say. I completely understand, and this book is going to prepare you to know *what you need and how to get it.* This is written for entry-level students of retirement planning—especially for those of us who may be rather reluctant students. I am speaking to you as an experienced professional, but my message comes straight from the heart of a woman who deeply understands how you are feeling and knows where you've been.

This is for women facing real-world retirement with real-time questions.

It's for women like you.

A NEW AND IMPROVED LIFE BEGINS TODAY

I applaud you for your willingness to read this, because doing so will help you avoid the mistakes I have made. With each chapter, you are going to have memories and feelings come up—these will be signals that you are ready for change. And change is what we need! By taking an active role in your own financial knowledge, you will reap tremendous benefits in all areas of your life. Increased confidence, better decision-making, peace of mind, improved health, a sense of empowerment, lessened stress and anxiety, and meaningful security will reward you for your time and effort. As a financially responsible and educated woman, you will be free to live life on your own terms, and quit living in constant fear of the unknown. It means that you'll know how to organize and prepare for a great future, and for anything that comes your way. It means that you're going to handle this!

It's time to get to work building something you can be proud of.

CHAPTER 2

WHY WOMEN

Not average—exceptional.

WOMEN ARE WIRED DIFFERENTLY

In the air, somewhere over Colorado, I heard a woman yell, "Somebody, please help me!" Seated next to Randy, I looked across the aisle of our thirty-seater plane to see that the massive turbulence had been too much for a brand-new mom: she had just thrown up all over her eight-week-old daughter. Panic filled her eyes, along with horrified embarrassment. We were on lock down for the plane's descent, and she was in no position to help her baby—or herself.

To Randy's shock, I reached past him for the baby girl, pulling the wailing vomit-laden infant across the aisle, across Randy's lap, and into my own.

Before her mother (or Randy, for that matter) could recover, a flight attendant yelled at me to put the baby back on the other side, as if shifting fifteen pounds across the aisle would bring down the whole plane. It was utterly ridiculous.

Without hesitation, a woman across the aisle (one seat in front of the sick mother) held out her arms, announcing, "Give her to me!" Back over Randy the reeking infant went, and her new custodian held her until the plane landed, allowing her mother time enough to tend to herself.

The plane touched down and the passengers scrambled to grab their baggage. The young mother scooped her baby up and rapidly deplaned—a puddle of embarrassment. Though she didn't thank me or even acknowledge those who had helped, it didn't trouble me—my reaction had been maternal and instinctive. It was the natural thing to do.

Randy, however, had difficulty trying to comprehend why I took the baby in the first place. He is a wonderful father to our three sons, but the idea of jumping into this lady's business was unfathomable.

Not so to a woman. What motivated me that day was one of the deepest and most mysterious parts of womanhood. It's something that women, young and old, exhibit—a deep desire to care for and protect those who are vulnerable. Women do this without hesitation, even to their own detriment.

> *"If I am not good to myself, how can I expect anyone else to be good to me?"* – MAYA ANGELOU

"AM I GOING TO BE OKAY?"

If this isn't the key question an advisor must answer every day, then I don't know what is. Women fundamentally want to know they are *going to be okay,* meaning they want financial security through their whole lives (freedom, options), and reassurance that they won't ever be a burden on their kids (those wonderful people they sacrificed years to care for). That's it. The deep concern in their hearts is, "Tell me I am going to be okay."

This may come across as a simple question, but it's not easy to answer. However, the ramifications of that answer can bring peace and solace to a woman's soul. Men will often have a to-the-point way of handling financial questions; they will want the details of an investment's projected rate of return, internal allocations, asset management strategy, etc. Women want the answers just as men do, but have a further desire to apply the issue on a personal level. Once the data is discussed, they want to know how it all applies specifically to them: "How is all of this going to help me be okay?"

Addressing these fears through proper planning can be an emotional process, filled with self-examination about core values and what truly matters. We need to talk through not only what you are planning to do, but *why*. Working with a financial advisor is not like speaking with a used car salesman—much the opposite, it is time spent preparing a woman's head and heart.

In Chapter One, I elaborated on how watching Randy gave me a compassionate perspective on how women should be treated in finance and led me to become a financial advisor. Yet, the further I dove into the financial industry in general, the more I observed that:

- Men and women typically had different financial needs
- The investment tools and methods for satisfying those needs were largely the same
- Most financial advisors I saw generally treated women as "small men" (whether they are male OR female advisors)
- Advisors often expected a woman to behave and plan like a man, and then became frustrated when she didn't fit the expectation
- Advisors often neglected women's emotional concerns and unique monetary needs

- Married women were often overlooked, as advisors predominantly addressed male spouses (even with both partners present)

I watched as Randy and our team—men and women—spoke with empathy about emotional subjects and how they intersect with money. And then I glanced around and saw that many others in our industry—again, men and women—approached planning in much the same way as the stereotypical scratching, belching, gorilla-like men on evening sitcoms, but with the bonus of being armed with spreadsheets.

Financial planning is very much about your core values. This is a message that is central to everything I do, and it's one I'll repeat until there's no longer breath in my lungs. You deserve better than a spreadsheet with projections. Just painting an invitation pink or adding some flowers doesn't make it female-friendly.

When Randy and I still owned our retirement planning firm, we worked with a team of financial advisors who were comfortable with women's emotions. Tears, hugs, and revelations were regular occurrences, and we were proud to provide an open and comfortable environment for female clients to feel completely safe to express themselves. After all, financial planning deals with real-life issues, and it was not uncommon to have a client drop an expletive or two in the middle of a personal conversations! This is the type of advisory relationship you need and deserve.

Safety. Security. Freedom of choice. Freedom of expression. Freedom to be wonderfully you.

Why would you expect anything less? You deserve to have, and feel, all these qualities. If you feel *less than* wherever you currently are, then shake that off and move on to where you'll be shown your worth. Keep looking for someone else.

The massive needs I saw around women's financial planning moved me to pivot our firm's focus years ago and specialize in serving this market. It also led me to my current vocation of training some of the most incredible, heart-forward, women-centric advisors across the nation through my company *LIFE with Arwen, Inc.* (www.arwenbecker.com). *Leaders Inspiring Financial Empowerment,* the origin of the *LIFE* acronym, is my effort to help other financial planners specifically focus their efforts on women in their communities. The meaning of the word *LIFE* evokes thoughts of growth, health, forward progress, and renewal—ideas we all benefit from when planning for our future.

ELDERLY POOR ARE MOSTLY FEMALE—TIME TO BE SELFISH

As I look back on my journey (or often, more accurately, "battle") with money, I marvel at my mom's willingness to sacrifice so much of her own comfort and future financial security to meet her daughters' needs. The more women I meet, regardless of age, the more universal this principle of self-sacrifice seems. My mom is one of the millions of selfless women who will do anything necessary to give their partners, children, grandchildren, and parents what they need—often at their own expense.

At the same time, strong women like her fear to ever be seen as a burden on their friends or extended family. It is a very perplexing dichotomy.

Women will sow all their seed and give away the harvest, yet never complain about their own lack of resources. Nor will they want to ask for assistance, to avoid being a bother. Sadly, though, it's often because of this deep desire to help loved ones that women surrender their financial security. You want others to be happy. You want them to have peace and not struggle. You want the very best for them. It is noble and beautiful to care for those who can't care for themselves, but we must be mindful of how it affects us.

"When you say, 'yes' to others, make sure you are not saying 'no' to yourself." – PAULO COELHO

Even more, caretaking requires an enormous amount of energy and time. It isn't just something we *do*, but rather, it becomes an entire lifestyle. Many women must take time off work—or leave employment completely—to prioritize their obligations. That's a tremendous risk, and it can bring serious economic hardship. Statistics show that the numbers of women in poverty far outweigh those of our male counterparts. It's not that men don't care, but they aren't genetically programmed to carry and nurture offspring in their own bodies, so there is something to be said about a woman's propensity to "mother."

Societal influences have told females, for centuries, that they are second-class citizens. It's only very recently that women gained any form of equality in western society, and if you are always considered "supporting, rather than starring," it's normal to put yourself on the back burner. So, we understand why we do it, but our gifts of compassion and care shouldn't compromise personal well-being!

I don't want that for you. You deserve better—you deserve safety. You deserve comfort. It's wonderful to see your loved ones happy, but must you endanger your own well-being? No. You know that.

Don't allow your love to make you a martyr. Please wake up and break whatever cycles are preventing you from having control of your own life (seek professional help if you feel stuck). Being selfless doesn't have to set you up to be broke at seventy-two. You won't win any extra life points by giving it all away.

You are too valuable. *You are.* Walk in that truth. Now, hold your head high and be very proud of yourself—you are amazing! Until now, you might have felt that you are in a corner, or even a dead-end. That's not so! There are solutions, opportunities, resources, blessings, and friends within near reach. This is only the beginning of the very best years of your life.

This is your time!

GO EASY ON YOURSELF—DON'T COMPARE TO OTHERS

Susan had been a client of ours for three years prior to her retirement. She had worked as a nurse for nearly forty years and was ready to retire. It was an exhausting job, and she was tired of the physical work, as well as being on her feet all day, the politics enveloping healthcare, and the massive changes that had occurred in the healthcare industry during her career. What she still enjoyed was the money, but the toll it took on her had become too much.

Susan was ready.

That Monday, she was giddy. It was her first official day of retirement, and she was eligible to roll over the remaining portion of her company retirement plan, her 403(b). Having entered our offices grinning ear to ear, she ordered her chai tea latte from our client concierge and walked down the hallway with great confidence. It was a tremendous experience for her, and she was excited for her new life chapter.

During our conference call with her 403(b) provider, we bantered gleefully, teasing the customer service rep, and laughing together, basking in Susan's joy of the moment. We scheduled a follow-up visit for the following Monday to finalize the last bits of her exit from working life.

The week passed, and Susan returned to our office for the next visit. But this time, she came with a look on her face that told a very different story. Something had changed. With a concerned welcome, I escorted her into the privacy of one of our conference rooms. She sat right down at the table, and I made my way to the other side asking, "Susan, how are things going?" Susan burst into tears, reached over to grab a tissue from the center of the table, and blurted out, "I was not ready for this. This is harder than I thought. I miss my friends!"

CHANGE IS BITTERSWEET

No matter how exciting your next season of life will be, you almost always leave something great behind.

It's much like raising kids. It is exciting to be done with diapers, but you miss the quiet snuggles of an infant lying against your chest. It is fantastic when that cute three-year-old toddler hangs on your every word, thinks you're a superhero, and screams with excitement when you walk through the front door. But later, that same innocent little angel will use your carefully-chosen home furnishings as a personal home art gallery. The little cherub will take a thick permanent marker and draw on your light-colored carpet, move towards the center of the stairs, and proudly finish coloring on his brother's crying face.

In retirement, you're happy to be done with the grind of being told what to do and when, and relieved of the pressure created by your workload. But we often have friends and routines that get left behind, and this can have you feeling awkward and idle. You may feel that you suddenly offer less value to the world around you. You feel a sense of loss. Grief.

I experienced this transition after we sold our retirement planning firm. I no longer had to wake to an alarm, get dressed to see my clients and employees, drive to an office, or think in terms of business hours Monday through Friday. My entire structure, and much of my perceived value, fell away instantly. The routine I had for decades was instantly eliminated. The fun team I had always had to socialize and plan with were no-more. So I can tell you that it is a tough process. It takes getting used to. You need to prepare your *future self* before you leave the workplace, to make sure that the massive shift doesn't overwhelm you. Many retirees spend the first two years in a sort of shellshock, wondering, "Now what?! Is this it?" As with anything, it can be hard to let go if you do not have a plan.

Go easy on yourself. Don't compare yourself to anyone else. They may be further along in their journey or have different values or goals. Most importantly, you must spend some quality time contemplating the meaningful work you want to do in your next season of life. You must have a vision beyond retirement.

> *"A (wo)man without vision will perish"* – PROVERBS 29:18

Build a vision board. Post pictures of the adventures or work you want to do. Consider hobbies, volunteering, consulting, or travel. Begin thinking about the value you will bring to others once you leave your formalized employment.

And while you may be completely thrilled to leave the nine-to-five world (or whatever kind of situation you have), leave room to let yourself grieve. You are bound to have mixed feelings once it actually happens. For a while, you might wonder if it was the right time to retire, or you might suddenly find yourself missing the co-worker you always seemed to despise. It's only natural! We are humans, and it takes time to accept any kind of change, even a good one.

This is your time to write your own story however you desire. Your canvas is blank, and you have every color in the palette, so let your paint fly! Get dirty! Don't let anyone else give you a paint-by-number. This is not their one life, it's yours. What have you always wanted to do? Why haven't you done it? How do you want to feel? What are you most excited to let go of? How will you make your ideas and dreams come true?

YOU MAY BE A FINANCIAL NINJA

The stories I tell and the situations I see are varied. I don't mean to imply with my message that women are inherently disengaged from their finances. I often sit with women who have a tremendous grasp of what's going in their financial lives. Maybe you are one of them and you understand your finances in full. Well done! Perhaps you're married, and you're the Financial Alpha who balances the checkbook and can tell what percentage your brokerage account earned last year.

One woman asked after an event, "I have owned a mortgage company, overseen my own investments all my life, and I've done well. What could you even do for me?"

I responded, "You have done what many women I meet with haven't; you have your finances all in line, so congratulations! Great job!" I smiled. "But one thing you have never done is retired anyone, including yourself. We've done it successfully for decades. The part I am most proud of is retiring people through the years of the Great Recession, and keeping them retired and peacefully enjoying life the way they want."

If that's who you are, partnering with an engaged retirement planner can take you from *good* to *great* in this unique season. You may be incredible at saving and accumulating assets. Still, I have seen some big mistakes made early in retirement that have devastating consequences when women apply the same game plan that got them to retirement. That plan might not get you through retirement. Let me repeat that in a different way; *the game and the rules change the moment you stop working.* Make sure you hire a coach (a.k.a. a financial advisor that specializes in retirement) to help you get it right from the very start, before you pull a hamstring or, worse, blow out a knee and perhaps even end your career (a.k.a. risk your financial peace in retirement).

Working with a specialized professional can and will make all the difference—and you don't have to work with *just anyone*. I will help you understand what an advisor does, and how he or she can be a tremendous advocate for your success. A good advisor does far more than talk numbers, and I will teach you how to make the most of that relationship.

So, whether you know every detail about your finances or are starting in a place of perceived ignorance and embarrassment, we are going to tackle this journey together. I have only one job to do, which is to leave you better than I found you. Please take this seriously, because no one deserves to be secure and happy more than you!

Let's do this!

> *Wisdom isn't something money can buy. It costs us time, effort, and focus.*

MOST IMPORTANT TAKEAWAYS

1. Women see and hear things differently. That's okay. You need an advisor who hears you and speaks to you in a way that YOU understand.

2. Women over age sixty-five have a greater likelihood of poverty[1]. Now that you're moving into proper planning, that statistic will not apply to you!

3. No one else can do the preparation for you (a.k.a. a man, the government, a parent).

NEXT STEPS

1. Say this out loud, "Starting right now, (list today's date) ___/___/_____, I will walk in my inherent value and worth! I can handle this!"

2. Continue to read this book to be empowered and inspired to tackle this important part of your life!

---

1 https://www.un.org/development/desa/dspd/2022/11/old-age-poverty/

CHAPTER 3

VALUES-BASED PLANNING

> *Today is all you've been promised—don't waste it.*

IS A COMPANY WORTH YOUR LIFE?

Boeing wants to be out of the pension business. As the world's largest aerospace company, they have begun offering many long-term employees a lump-sum pension buyout, hoping to end their days as a long-term pension provider. Dick was one of those fortunate employees. He enlisted our help to determine whether to leave the retirement funds at Boeing for them to distribute to him as a lifetime pension, or to take it as a lump sum.

Dick was seventy-one and had dedicated forty-three years to this extraordinary and world-changing company.

He came in for an initial visit with his wife, who was a few years younger and vibrant. She had a bubbly attitude and colorful fashion sense. They were thrilled to start enjoying retirement together—she had already waited ten years after her own retirement for Dick to be "ready."

Their retirement funds were healthy. Dick was not. As I watched Dick leave my office that day following our meeting, I knew something was not right. He struggled to get out of the chair and put his coat back on. As I observed him shuffle out of my office, my heart sank. All I could hear in my head was the question on repeat, "Was Boeing worth it?"

The weeks rolled into months as Dick and Alice transitioned into retirement. They moved into a new retirement community, made fast friends, and went on their first trip as a dually retired couple (a cruise to the Caribbean!). During their next visit to our office, Alice marveled at how much fun it was and couldn't wait for their next trip to Europe together. They were getting accustomed to their new retired life.

Sadly, that next trip would never come.

Dick had been retired less than two years when he slipped while walking the dog. He had a fall that seriously injured his head. He stumbled back to their house, where Alice called for an ambulance.

As Dick was going in and out of consciousness, the staff at the intensive-care unit did what they could to stabilize him. Twenty-four hours after being admitted, in a near-miraculous moment of lucidity, Dick called for his wife. They enjoyed a thirty-minute loving conversation. Dick told Alice once more of his deep and loving devotion to her. He said that he had the most wonderful life with her, and that she was his everything. Dick died an hour later.

When Alice called us to let us know that he had passed, my heart sank for the second time. I didn't want to be right, but when you work for decades with retirees, you see patterns. Dick had given forty-three years of his most productive and healthy years to a company. He generated nearly two million dollars in retirement savings. And for what? Less than two years of retirement.

Disappointingly, this happens all the time. Many people are motivated to work far longer than necessary, because they fear that they won't have enough money to retire. This kind of pressure pushes people like Dick to give the best of themselves to their company, rather than to their family and/or personal dreams.

Dick had waited too long to truly live, leaving his lovely bride to walk retirement by herself.

One popular quote rings true: *"People spend their health trying to gain wealth and then often spend their wealth trying to regain health."* Dick's carefully planned wealth could do nothing to buy back the healthy years that too much work had stolen. You have one trip around this planet and one body to do it in. Work out. Walk daily. Hire a nutritionist for a visit or two (you don't need dozens of visits to learn a lot). Read a health book. Buy a fitness tracker watch. Keep your health in check and *please,* don't give the best of you to a company. Your family deserves that gift, and you want to spend as much time with them as possible—while you are still active and healthy. I want to motivate you create the plan that's best for you and get you in the right mental space, so you can enjoy life *before and after* retirement.

THE BEST YEARS OF YOUR LIFE—THE GO-GO YEARS

Multiple studies have been done that state the best years of your life are between the ages of sixty and seventy-five. Hands down.

By this time, you know yourself. You have the wisdom of experience. You've got money. You've got time. If you're married, your spouse is likely still living. You aren't competing with the Joneses any longer. Your friends are still around—and now, they have more free time. The grandkids are young enough that they still want to spend time with you. You've got your best health. You're able to go out and do things that you have been patiently waiting to do. You've got dreams...

These are called the *Go-Go Years*.

Many of you reading this are older than seventy-five and still very much in the Go-Go mindset. That is wonderful. I've worked with many eighty-year-olds who are vivacious, busy, and traveling. Conversely, many of you may be in your late forties, but you emphasize the importance of deliberately enjoying your life *right now*. I commend you. That is what we all ought to be doing—living our best life now. Tomorrow isn't guaranteed for any of us, and with every day that passes, health may dictate what we can and can't do.

I am trying to stir up those of you who, like Dick, are too afraid that you "won't have enough for the future" if you take some time right now to relish the life and the finances you have worked so hard to put into place. You've been laboring your entire life. Please don't wait; get educated, meet with a retirement planner and, with help, create a way to love your life now while planning correctly for your future.

> *"Don't wear yourself out. Don't work yourself to the bone. Wealth is fleeting—it's just not worth killing yourself in a bid to acquire more and more."* – PROVERBS 23:4-5

Spend now! Seriously? That's a tall order, considering that you've worked at accumulating and saving for the last thirty to forty years. This may be the toughest hurdle you'll face nearing or just entering retirement. You must trust your advisor's assessment and believe what the mathematical planning process says. What have you been dreaming to do? Why are those dreams still on hold? It's time to start putting a dollar figure on those dreams and putting those goals into action! Solid and holistic planning can clearly demonstrate whether your life-long financial efforts will give you enough money to retire comfortably and cover the *what-ifs* (unknown span of life, future healthcare needs, a repeat of the Great Recession, etc.). Therefore, plan your retirement, and then let yourself enjoy life—every single day.

> *"What are you going to do with this one wild and precious life?"*
> – MARY OLIVER

MATH DOESN'T LIE

You've likely heard the term *return on investment* (ROI). For example: an advisor sits with you, bragging about how their investments posted a 10 percent average ROI over the past couple of years. *Oh, sounds good, right?* Maybe you're thinking, "Math doesn't lie," and you'd be right. But, in the same way that your teacher always checked your work, when someone starts talking about averages, you should always look deeper.

For instance, if a couple jogs an average of twenty-five miles a week, you'd envision both people rising at the crack of dawn to zip on their tracksuits. But what if that average instead means that one of them gets up when it's still dark and jogs ten miles every weekday morning for a total of 50 miles, while the other one stays in their pajamas and plays cat-and-mouse with the snooze button?

Let's see how the game of averages breaks down with ROI.

	SCENARIO ONE – MORE RISK/VOLATILITY		SCENARIO TWO – LESS RISK/VOLATILITY	
Year 0		$1,000,000		$1,000,000
Year 1 ROI	60 percent ROI	Add: $600,000	30 percent ROI	Add: $300,000
Total after Year 1:		$1,600,000		$1,300,000
Year 2 ROI	-40% ROI	Minus: $640,000	-10% ROI	Minus: $130,000
Total after Year 2:		$960,000		$1,170,000
Total ROI after 2 years:		10%		10%
10% ROI	60% - 40% = 20% divide by 2 years		30% - 10% = 20% divide by 2 years	

	SCENARIO ONE – EMOTIONAL ROLLER COASTER		SCENARIO TWO – RELAXED	
Year 0		$1,000,000		$1,000,000
Year 1 ROI	15% ROI	Add: $150,000	8% ROI	Add: $80,000
Total after Year 1:		$1,150,000		$1,080,000
Year 2 ROI	-7% ROI	Minus: $80,500	0% ROI	Minus: $0
Total after Year 2:		$1,069,500		$1,080,000
Total ROI after 2 years:		4%		4%
4% ROI	15% - 7% = 8% divide by 2 years		8% - 0% = 8% divide by 2 years	

Examples are shown for illustrative purposes only and don't reflect taxes or investment fees.

Again, we have two portfolios with the same average ROI. Math doesn't lie. If you have the same ROI, but less volatility (the range in which the positive and negative numbers swing), you will always have more money in the end. It's pure mathematics, and it reduces your degree of worry. If you're constantly striving for 10 percent, 12 percent, or more, but it's causing unnecessary volatility and an unending emotional roller coaster, it isn't worth it. Period.

When creating a retirement projection that goes into your plan, don't assume any ROIs higher than 7 percent—even with our most aggressive professionally managed growth portfolios, we never included anything in a long-term plan higher than 7 percent. Doing so would be irresponsible when running long-range scenarios. Instead, it's vital to show that your retirement could function well if your assets earn 3 percent to 7 percent (maximum) with the added pressure of high inflation rates (3 percent or more) and low *cost-of-living adjustments* (COLAs) on your Social Security. You do this to *pressure test* your retirement plan from every direction. Make it strain and struggle under the conservative weight of it all. That way, you can maintain a sense of confidence that your plan would work beautifully as you continue to manage your expenses as you have been.

MATH AND RESPONSIBILITY COLLIDE

What if you could have that same standard of living and lifestyle with less volatility, and enjoy a less stressful retirement? Wouldn't that feel a lot better? That is called *return on retirement* (ROR). Return on Retirement is a phrase created by fourteen-time best-selling author David Bach, and it is a brilliant twist on the standard focus of ROI.

RETURN ON RETIREMENT (ROR)

Financial Guru and prolific best-selling author David Bach coined the phrase *Return on Retirement* and I love the idea behind it. Let's look at the difference between ROI and ROR. Many advisors will talk about moving the money you have around in stocks, bonds, mutual funds, ETFs, REITs, variable annuities, indexed annuities, life insurance, etc. These are all tools, but they aren't a plan. A great advisor will help you plan for, with an acceptable degree of certainty, a retirement in which all the money you've saved during your working years provides for your entire life (especially for you married women). They will help you organize a strategy to cover your income needs, your future healthcare, or the death of a spouse, as well as the dreams you've been waiting to fulfill once you retire. That last piece seems to be one that some advisors frequently overlook in the planning process.

You aren't here to "time the market" or chase returns. You're building a comprehensive plan based on conservative rates of expected return that helps you keep the money piece in the background and your best years in the foreground. That's what you should be striving for, and that's what you deserve after your years of hard work and sacrifice. The most important part of your planning is making sure that the dreams you have come with a dollar figure attached to each element and are illustrated and woven into your plan.

The beauty of retirement is that it's your time and you can do what you want, when you want, however you choose. So relish in your dreams and make sure you have a solid financial foundation to make those desires happen! Life is to be enjoyed!

There is a big difference between investing versus planning, and the same applies to ROI versus ROR.

FOUNDATIONAL PILLARS OF A RETIREMENT PLAN

Many Americans let fear guide their financial decisions. I can understand why, since money feels like such a scarce and delicate commodity for so many people. I have been there in the biggest way. I get it. You may be afraid of losing in the market, or concerned that you won't have enough income. Perhaps you're bothered by the idea of losing purchasing power to inflation. Those are the central points that financial advisors help people address every day. Common sense and wise planning help us move past those stringent financial fears.

As we are building a well-fortified structure of retirement, it needs to have very specific foundational pillars that are laid out in a very distinct order. When you are in your twenties, thirties, and early forties, these are reversed. But as we approach retirement (with more working years behind us than in front of us), we moved towards fixed income. This means that we are no longer working and earning a paycheck, and these pillars shift to reduce the anxiety of financial money management.

PRESERVATION OF ASSETS

The first pillar as you approach retirement is *preservation of assets*. You've worked your entire life to accumulate your retirement funds. You need to make sure that at least a portion of that money is protected, and that those assets will be there throughout the rest of your beautiful existence (not just for ninety percent of your life).

INCOME PLANNING

The second pillar is *income planning*. Many of you will experience an income gap once you *separate from service* (stop working) and are no longer collecting regular wages. The gap might be even more significant if you retire in your fifties or early sixties, as Social Security or Medicare hasn't yet kicked in and you're paying hefty premiums for health insurance (and other such related costs). You need to find a way to create a guaranteed regular income while helping you to enjoy the fun times that early retirement affords you.

GROWTH

The third pillar is *growth*. Growth is still a vital component of your retirement plan—especially as a woman—because that is what helps guard against the risks of longevity, inflation, and the cost of future healthcare. Growth can also help you leave a meaningful legacy to those you love. What we don't want is for growth to threaten the first two pillars, which are *preservation of your assets* and *income*. *When you* are in your early working years, growth is the most important pillar. You have time to make up a loss and decades of compounding interest. Yet, as we age, a loss can become more detrimental and compounding interest loses much of the power it once had. By putting growth in its proper place, third place once we near retirement, we can invest for the future without having to micromanage all the ways that tomorrow's market movement might affect your bill-paying abilities, and more importantly, your peace of mind.

IDENTIFY YOUR VALUES

The best way to facilitate and simplify the decision-making process is to first identify your core values. These will be your priorities, what matters deepest in your soul, and they are the factors we consider when facing life choices. Our values help to guide our motivation behind the decisions we make, giving us the *why* to everything we do. Each person's priorities are unique and personal, and they give us a sense of purpose in life.

> *"Be thankful for what you have; you'll end up having more. If you concentrate on what you don't have, you will never, ever have enough."*
> – OPRAH

Just like planning in a micro-climate (more on this idea in Chapter Six), I often see women decide how to spend their money without considering their bigger picture, or their values. It is essential to discover and acknowledge the values you carry in your heart and soul, and make your financial choices match up with those directions, rather than creating a "value" to justify your spending habits (that always leaves you feeling empty and unsatisfied).

This exercise is essential to the whole planning process because you want to make sure that anything that is used, any investments or products, has purpose and focus. It's critical that your financial plan is built on your core values—meaning the big picture of life, not just the next hot investment.

I am speaking about the intangibles (values): freedom, comfort, not being a burden on your family, choices, security, good health, independence, spirituality, education, friendship, community, service, etc. Not the tangibles (goals): travel, boat, new car, golf, a gated-community home in Arizona, etc.

Such goals are all wonderful and exciting, but they are not values. If you set your attention on making choices that honor your priorities of family and good heath, you might decide that travel is a good option. You might take your grandchildren for a week to the lake in the mountains, where there is fresh air and less stress. That serves the value of family, defined by your desire to travel. There is a great *why* behind that trip! If you put your focus only on the tangibles, you will be left with a searching soul and your long-term financial security may be threatened.

Values last, and they matter. Values cannot be bought or sold, and they do not disappear when the market goes low. If one of your core values is compromised, the goal or goals get canceled. Values should dictate every decision.

This exercise is important for all, and particularly vital for couples. The majority of divorces stem from money disputes. Getting on the same page, value-wise—even if it means upsetting the apple cart a bit to dig into your household finances—can make a difference in the longevity of both your savings and your relationship. A little discomfort today can mean comfort for decades into the future (oh boy, do I know this truth all too well).

For those of you who are married to a woman, getting on the same page is vitally important to the long-term health of your relationship. Most same-sex couples we worked with still had differing opinions surrounding risk and reward, so this premise still applies. However, in our practice, we normally saw greater discrepancies between men and women, their differing mindsets, and emotional approaches. Certainly, some men are more in touch with their emotions, and some women struggle to access theirs, but for now I'm going to elaborate on what we'd see as a *typical* contrast of men's and women's planning.

Seeing and understanding the intangibles is often a lot easier for women since they are naturally more connected to their emotions and feelings, whereas men may have to work a bit harder to get to that same root. But don't be fooled; men have very strong emotions, yet they may need a bit more time to think and meditate on what money means to them, since most of them have grown up being goal-focused. Be patient.

When I speak at financial events, I ask the audience, "What does money mean to you?" It is uncanny that about 99 percent of the time, women throw out words in the values/intangibles category, and men throw out goals and tangibles.

Men are just wired differently.

OOPS, I DID IT AGAIN

When I went to work for Randy after my divorce, I had a monthly check from my ex in payment for my half of our community property, my paycheck from my job, and a tiny bit coming in from my side hustle with Amway. I thought I was rollin' in the dough! Yet, I still wasn't educating myself about finance as it might apply to me.

Just like my former partner, Randy had all the trappings of success and had experienced his fair share up to that point. I felt that I had it made (again)! However, anyone who's launched a business without seed money from rich parents or an inheritance, knows the first few years can be very tough—especially when those first three years of a financial company fall squarely into the *Dot Bomb* era. His role was making the money for the business, and I aggressively supported that, doing my part by managing employees, planning financial seminars, running the administrative aspects meticulously, and executing the business accounting. I learned very quickly that new businesses suck money and often there was too much month at the end of the money. So to help, I stopped collecting a paycheck when we got engaged, figuring it was the right thing to do.

What I failed to see was that only a few years after my divorce, I had begun to slide back into "white knight" syndrome. Sure, I was dipping my feet into the pool of finance—though at that point I was not an advisor in any capacity—but I hadn't taken ownership of my money or my circumstances. I relied one hundred percent on Randy for that.

As I mentioned before, I was reading all the touchy-feely books on confidence, excellence, love, and faithfulness, but I never cracked even one book concerning money. I knew the basics of personal financial planning from a theoretical standpoint, of course, but that was still largely the realm of Randy. With fifteen years of experience at that time (now he has thirty-nine!), he was an impressive financial advisor. Why would I need to bother with our financial details? He'd take care of those things, right?

Randy's upbringing was very different from my own. His dad was an accountant who scraped to take care of Randy's mother through her battle with debilitating Multiple Sclerosis. My mom was a lunch lady who did her best to be mother, father, protector, disciplinarian, chauffeur, cook, and clean-up crew for my sister and me (and my alcoholic stepdad). We lived in the negative space left by both my father's and stepdad's various failings and mistakes. Teaching us about saving, investing, entrepreneurship, and the like was not on that list.

I was a math whiz and took statistics in college just because I enjoyed it. But I didn't know anything about running a business, principal and interest, cash flow, taxation, or any of the rest of it. I thought I knew "enough." Some of it was arrogance (It's not that hard, right? I'm smart. If I need to know something, I'll figure it out), and some of it was regular neglect (I am young, I'll figure it out "tomorrow").

KNOWLEDGE IS POWER AND CONFIDENCE

Finance isn't a particularly thrilling or glamorous topic—at least, not at first glance. We women are busy, and we barely have enough time to get dinner on the table, let alone figure out trends in the stock market and how that may affect our long-term financial strategy. Learning about money doesn't generally feel like something we'd be excited to do in our downtime. You'd be hard-pressed to find any thrilling television dramas about female financial advisors. However, when we stop and consider the true benefits of understanding personal finance, it's a different story altogether.

Finance is far more than numbers. Familiarize yourself just a little, and you'll start to see that it's about choices—and freedom. It's a personalized path of empowerment, prioritization, family, confidence, and security for the future. Stereotypically, we often think that dealing with money is just an onerous task—or a boring chore.

We're tired enough already, right? Besides, we don't want to upset anyone. Our spouse might think we are ungrateful or questioning their financial prowess if we try to take ownership of our finances or ask too many questions.

Sometimes, women don't look at money because they simply don't want to know. They will spend without checking their bank account, shove receipts into drawers, use one credit card after the other, and just keep busy until they absolutely must go and speak with the teller. They simply find it too stressful to even think about the numbers. Have you ever gone to the grocery store and held your breath while the debit card is processing? Instead of knowing where they are with money, they "assume" and "hope." That's a very stressful way to live. It's like burying your head in the sand to avoid the sun.

Men are allowed to talk about money—they are encouraged to do so. It's a very manly thing to wear a suit and walk into a bank, briefcase in hand. When they discuss money, we see them as successful, intelligent, and ambitious. They are leaders and decision-makers (sadly it wasn't more than a generation ago when a woman couldn't open a bank account on her own without her husband there to co-sign). When women talk about money, our society traditionally views them as greedy, shallow, or even *out of their league*. And we always must fight the age-old superstition that women are "bad at math." Men are taught to be enterprising, and women are told to be *nice*.

These excuses are all too common. But keeping the peace is of little comfort when consequence comes knocking.

GREAT RECESSION HIT HARD

The worst stock market decline in my life, second worst to the Great Depression, struck in September 2008. Nearly everyone reading this book was affected in one way or another during that downturn, and it rattled the worldwide economy. People lost jobs, homes, possessions, and the feeling of personal worth that goes with those things. There are many kinds of life events that can be planned for, and thoughtful advisors carefully build those into every financial plan. Our clients' accounts were no exception.

An economic recession affects us financially, as well as emotionally. Randy and I owned a firm that managed wealth, and we were positioned to be a rock of stability for our clients—especially when they felt the stress of helplessness in a down market. It wasn't pleasant to see clients facing their worst fears, sleepless and anxious from the barrage of bad national news. During the 2008 recession, most of our clients fared well because preservation of their assets was always our primary focus (recall the three pillars: preservation, income, and *then growth*), so much of their assets had been moved into risk-free investments, not direct market exposure. Much of our time was dedicated to consulting clients on an emotional level and helping them to remain strong and calm (and not make an irrational financial move) amidst all the craziness that we were seeing around us.

Yet with something as massive as the Great Recession, it was only inevitable that when the tide went out, all boats would go down. There was less overall wealth for us to manage. We were counseling our dear clients and pushing ourselves to the limit, feeling the hurt. Our priority was to take care of our clients and our employees. However, there was too much happening at once. We couldn't keep doing business as usual because the definition of "usual" had completely changed.

Long-term clients were struggling with "analysis paralysis," afraid of making any course corrective changes in their retirement plans during 2009, so simple phone calls with our clients to take our advice, like we'd had in the past, were halted due to fear. New client acquisition dried up as financial prospects sat tight. Our revenue dwindled by 66 percent from 2008 to 2010, causing our personal and business debt to balloon to an agonizing and debilitating $675,000—

we were experiencing the Great Recession's ricochet effect. Our clients were managing alright, but Randy and I had shifted into total emergency mode to protect them, our company, and our employees. The economic crisis hit home, and something had to give.

That *something* was our personal residence, and, after eighteen months and three failed attempts to renegotiate our home loan, we entered foreclosure proceedings.

Failure.

NUDE AND HUMILIATED

You might be asking yourself, "What do I have to learn from a financial advisor who was foreclosed on and in massive debt following the Great Recession?" If you put this book down and walk away, or at least scratch your head in confusion—I don't blame you.

But please, as they say, *don't leave before the miracle happens.*

Dear Reader, I've had some serious low points. I laughed somewhat desperately through my tears at a bank employee trying to collect on our non-existent auto loan payment, saying, "well, the good news is you can't repo my kids!" I'll never forget distressingly borrowing money from our twelve-year-old to gas up the car, right before Christmas 2010.

I'll be the first to put up a hand if someone asks, "Who has ever been foolish about money?"

Yet: "Let him who is without sin among you be the first to throw a stone at her (John 8:7 NIV)." When multiple men dragged a nude, humiliated woman out into the public square, having caught her in adultery, they wanted Jesus to condemn her to death by stoning her. That would have been the appropriate legal punishment in those ancient times. I'm going to set the justice system of 30 A.D. aside (as well as the ludicrous double-standard that allowed the adulterous man to remain anonymous), and instead face the fact that this adulterous woman made a terrible choice, no question. But redemption is always possible *if someone is willing to change.* Jesus' response was not to excuse her infidelity, but to make everyone holding their rocks, judging her, instead stand in judgment of themselves. Under the weight of their own internal examination of their own lives, they all failed. Everyone dropped their rocks, starting with the oldest (and wisest) among them.

We all fail. And we are called to change. I also realized that hearts don't just break, they also mend. For years after that I was grieving a loss, the loss of the home where our youngest son, Easton, took his first earthly breaths. Why, God, did you take that away from me? What did I do wrong? I couldn't let go of the loss and move forward. I struggled to find joy in others getting their dream home (or quite honestly, just owning a home, condo or place of their own). It took me years (yes, years) to finally accept the loss and realize that home that overlooked the golf course Randy and I were married in was never coming back. I decided to finally move forward and stop looking back. This experience of what I saw as a complete financial life failure was my call to do what many women the world over have done since the dawn of humanity: **I (finally) handled it.**

MISTAKES ARE A PART OF LIFE

What is the biggest financial mistake you have ever made? What feelings do you still have about that mistake? What if I told you that *failure* was the door to open your greatest potential? When we learn from our mistakes and grow, how can they truly be called mistakes?

Honestly, many women make financial *mistakes* because they follow someone else's advice and desires. Or maybe they do what they think they *should* do, instead of learning the facts and trusting their own reasoning. The real mistake is not taking responsibility and working without enough information.

Randy and I both recognized the need for change in our own financial lives, and so we began the hard and harrowing work of transformation, side by side. No more blaming and fault-finding. It was work that not only saved our business, but transformed our marriage, our family, our attitudes, and our lives forever.

We moved fast and made prompt modifications, reading personal finance books, having late-night conversations, attending couples therapy, making spreadsheets and checklists, doing meditations, purging belongings and unnecessary expenses, taking classes, and making use of business and financial coaches. In seven years (yep, seven: it takes longer to fill a financial hole than it does to create one), we went from a highly leveraged business carrying hundreds of thousands in tax obligations and debt, to owning a home and two rental properties. Except for our mortgages, we became totally debt-free in our personal and professional lives. We fully funded our retirements, insurance policies, college 529 savings plans, began to truly live the adage of *pay yourself first,* and had three months of emergency expenses set aside (three is the minimum you should have; now we have twelve, which is ideal). I began to walk, well-educated, alongside my husband, instead of expecting him to carry me on his back. We were like two oxen, yoked up and pulling the weight equally, in unison and in the same direction.

By implementing new ways of thinking *in the small things,* they compounded into huge, sweeping changes *in all things.*

During my latter career, I had been dismissed as a financial advisor by prospective clients who found the public records about our foreclosure. I am not ashamed: *we learned.* We forfeited our personal home to make sure we maintained our business, which included the most important commitments to our clients and employees. I am proud, looking back, of the way we chose to continue as a company to serve our community, even if we suffered severe personal setbacks. God has more than returned all that we financially lost during those years! The sacrifice proved to be worth it as we sold our twenty-two-year financial planning firm in 2022 and ushered in our own retirement dreams! The biggest thing I took away from all those years of clawing out of that hole is, it is okay to want to quit—*just don't!* Our lives are beautiful testament to not quitting on yourself even though it may take years (or even decades) to realize your dream.

Randy and I humbled ourselves and got educated in areas where we were falling short. You are doing the same thing now, in choosing to read this book: shining light on the darkness. You go, girl!

MONEY THERAPIST

As we read one of my favorite books, *Smart Couples Finish Rich,* by David Bach (his other book, *Smart Women Finish Rich,* is perfect for the single gals and nearly the exact same book), we discovered two eye-opening things: one, we had an eighteen-point to-do list of things that we needed to tackle or update in our own financial lives, and two, we each saw our money from very different points of view (here's a little side note: if we as two financial advisors had eighteen things we needed to work on in our own financial lives, imagine how many things you will discover when you dive in deeply into your finances, too).

My opinion and Randy's opinion of how to handle our finances were deeply rooted in our respective childhoods and personal histories. Authors of financial books act as *money therapists,* and financial advisors fill that role as well, to help you get to the root of what matters and then focus your plan around those priorities. In our own lives, we had to clearly identify what we each valued about our money, and then combine the two sets of values to anchor ourselves when making financial decisions (big or small).

Sorry if I come across as a broken record, but the most important aspect of your planning is to determine your values. Now.

I'm serious. *Right now!*

Do. Not. Delay.

I've sat down with too many women that were contemplating divorce over a fundamental difference in the way each spouse approached money. It's awful. If Randy and I had continued our path, without seeking sage advice from financial counselors and business owners, it might have destroyed our marriage as well. That is not going to be you. Don't passively sit back and wait. Get focused, deliberate, and diligent on this money piece. You and your partner need to clearly identify what your values are by doing this upcoming exercise separately. The next step will be to combine your responses into one list of solid values that makes both of you feel heard and puts you in agreement.

If a couple is not in harmony, at the very least, life will carry turmoil and uncertainty. But in the worst case, the marriage will end because of money disagreements. No one wants that. Not your kids, your grandkids, or your friends, so it is worth a bit of being uncomfortable and tackling this often-difficult subject of money and values. Hire a marriage therapist of you need help here. A handful of quarrels are much easier to deal with than a divorce, and they're a lot less costly (emotionally, mentally, and financially).

I urge you to get this done in the next couple of weeks because it makes the entire planning process a lot easier. Financial issues can be very hard on a married couple because it tends to hit as a "you versus me" and "wrong or right" dynamic. Neither of those are true, and there are two very wonderful and unique individuals trying to have a serious conversation. First thing is to step back and understand the problem before you go hard into taking sides. You are both on the same team, with a loving shared goal of freedom and security.

I believe in you, and your relationship is worth it!

GETTING TO THE CORE OF THE MATTER

Stop here! Grab a pencil or pen.

I really don't want you to go any further in this book without taking a few minutes to do this exercise. Find a pencil and start filling in the blanks right in the pages of this book (or, if you are reading this on an e-reader, grab a journal or piece of paper).

This exercise is the start to changing your life. You are ready for this part of the book, because I know that you want to change. You want something better for yourself and your life. *You can handle this.*

Now ask yourself, "What does money mean to me? What are the feelings I sense when I think about having money in my accounts?" Checkmark, highlight, star, circle, or whatever you prefer, to denote those that matter most to you.

Note: If you are married, take a photo of this list before you begin your work, then your spouse will have their list to view without your answers on it. You can then compare your responses.

- Security
- Control
- Freedom
- Fun
- Safety
- Options
- Personal strength
- Power
- Influence
- Peace
- Good health
- Not being a burden on my kids
- Time with my family
- Time with my friends
- Ability to volunteer

▲ _____ (write here)

▲ Think some more. Probe deeper for anything not on the list.

▲ _____ (write here)

▲ _____ (write here)

▲ _____ (write here)

(If you are part of a couple, STOP HERE. Do not complete the top five below until your spouse/partner has done their own list)

Now I want you to list your top five core values below. If you do this as a couple, show each other what you wrote and discuss the best way to blend those values into a list of five.

My/our top five core values are:

1. _____ (write here)

2. _____ (write here)

3. _____ (write here)

4. _____ (write here)

5. _____ (write here)

These five should speak directly to the core of what matters to you. When you say them out loud, these words should evoke feelings deep inside that help you to feel content and secure. As you close your eyes and imagine those words, a sense of peace and inspiration should wash over you. That feeling is what we need to help you make sound financial decisions based on material in the remainder of this book.

With each new situation, ask yourself, "Does this financial decision get me closer to those five core values, or move me further away?" If it is the latter, you'll want to make a different choice. Let your values be your guide.

Now that you have the most important piece identified, it's time to rock this thing called life!

> *At any moment, you can choose a fresh start.*

MOST IMPORTANT TAKEAWAYS

1. Return on Retirement (ROR) is what you are seeking. It's about peace of mind more than Return on Investment (ROI).

2. We all fall short at times, but "getting back up" is always your choice.

3. When you identify your core values, making financial decisions becomes a lot simpler.

4. 4Couples need to identify core values to gain an understanding of what matters most to both partners and how your core values compare.

NEXT STEPS

1. Run through the values exercise before going on to the next chapter. If you need to wait for a partner/spouse, determine what date you will have it done by: ___/___/_____.

2. Take these top five values and write them, right now, in ink on the inside front cover of this book (or put a little card in your wallet), so you can easily access what really matters to you when faced with financial decisions.

CHAPTER 4

GOOD NEWS

> *Stop comparing your blooper reel with others' highlight reel.*

NO MORE HAIR NETS

"Oh my God, what if it doesn't work?" These words swirled around the mind of a careful, calculating, and hard-working mother of two. Once my mom hit forty-three, and both my sister and I had graduated from high school, she admitted that she'd had enough of living paycheck to paycheck. She was ready for a fresh start.

My father was tens of thousands behind in child support, and even more so in meaningful visits, yet she knew it would be fruitless trying to collect or hiring costly attorneys (or bad-mouthing him to us). She just got up and went to work. Every single day. She was at work by 5 a.m., preparing food for a bunch of ungrateful junior high kids and slaving away in a hot kitchen. Mom was on her aching feet all day to earn a measly paycheck and be home by 2:30 p.m. so her daughters had a mom around for homework, chores, athletics, and attention.

My stepdad did little to assist in making her life any easier. In fact, he largely complicated an already heavy load, as he was unwilling to pay taxes, work a legitimate job and pay into Social Security, or take care of much of the household expenses. Mom made dinner, managed the household, raised us girls, shuttled me to hundreds of hours of practices and games, and kept the house as tidy as she could. Financially, she bore nearly all the responsibility. She hustled to pay rent and put food on the table while he ran up a high tab of irresponsibility. For nearly five years, the government even garnished her wages to take care of a loan he was unwilling to pay. My mom had a deep well of energy, but much of that vigor was spent trying to put out his fires. She was truly a survivor.

Finally, she was looking at a job opportunity beyond the school cafeteria. But would there be any chance for redemption? Heck yes! She is a woman. She is a mother. She is a warrior. She saved and sacrificed. She handled it.

She declared, "Enough is enough." With both of us girls out of the house, she took a leap of faith and left the lunchroom for a seasonal job at a local Costco. There were no guarantees. It meant a pay cut with a longer commute and no benefits. But she rolled the dice.

Since her only occupational experience was in food service, they put her to work during the 1998 holiday season in the little food court at the Costco adjacent to their corporate office in Issaquah, Washington. She was exhausted from doing that kind of labor. She certainly didn't love the job, and it was grueling work that had her on her feet all day. But those were the skills that she had. Mom was tenacious and confident enough to believe her work ethic would shine so brightly that they wouldn't dare think to let her go once the Christmas season was over.

Jackpot! Well, sort of.

Costco couldn't live without her, this was true. She was a gem. Mom was the kind of employee you pray to add to your team. She was the player who inspired everyone around her to work a bit harder, longer, and with greater integrity. The company formalized her employment to full-time in the food court, and eventually promoted her to manager. It was her first step up the ladder, and that, alone, was important.

It was never her lifelong intention to prepare mass amounts of giant pizzas or grilled Polish dogs. She had plenty enough to do at home, let alone clean trash from large metal tables or take care of the messes left by careless suburban teenagers after they scarfed down their cheap eats. But she stayed faithful to the course she believed in. My mother was certainly no quitter!

JACKPOT!

After one full year doing this kind of thankless work, Mom put in an application for a higher position with Costco, pulled the Vegas slots lever, and rolled the magical triple 7s.

"Donna, we're offering you a position in the corporate office," they responded. It meant no more hair nets! How many years had she worked behind food service tables, only to finally be recognized! My mother had never complained or eyed the proverbial corner office, but her integrity bank account would finally pay off.

With the thousands and thousands of employees Costco has, I doubt they could find many other employees who are more honest, hardworking, and consistent as my mom. And talk about faithfulness! She was married to my stepdad for 45 years, and in the final year of his battle with lung cancer (he passed in 2021), she paid $9,000/month out of pocket to cover his nursing home (since he hadn't paid into Social Security, he couldn't receive Medicare benefits).

Until the bitter end, my mom bore the financial weight of his choices; she handled it. So imagine the immense joy when we all saw my mom retire from Costco in 2022 after working in their corporate office for twenty-four years! She built up an incredible retirement account out of diligence, consistent savings, and dollar-cost averaging (I'll address DCA in Chapter Seven).

Even without child support (she was, for decades, the primary blue-collar breadwinner), she achieved financial peace amid the dysfunction and dishonesty instigated by my stepdad, and a late start. Rather than wringing her hands, getting mad, or hiding her head in the sand, she took responsibility and made things happen. Not every woman has a partner to depend on, and many find themselves in situations like hers that are far more complicated than just being a single mom or widow.

However, let me point out one thing my mom had that most women don't: *she had a daughter and son-in-law that were financial advisors.* She sought our direction. She listened to our advice. She got honest about her money and the problems my stepdad was creating. The biggest lesson is she was coachable; my mom acted upon our advice and reviewed her plan every year (even with the dysfunction going on in the background, she didn't wait till everything was perfect—she began right where she was). She didn't make excuses or cry victimhood, she just rolled up her sleeves and did the work.

My mom is a stellar example of female courage. Mothers, daughters, and sisters are often overwhelmed with caretaking and family duties, so they put themselves last. She may have put her fun and joy on the back burner, but she stayed focused on her long-term plan of eventually retiring. She knew the little things added up and assistance from an advisor was deeply beneficial. This is where many women falter—neglecting to ask for help. We give 101 percent to everyone else and neglect our own needs, which leaves us vulnerable and exhausted. "Just keep going" seems far more important than setting boundaries or getting one's needs met.

We all know a woman like my mom who works hard, keeps her head down, and handles it. The problem is that they often don't understand their true worth, because they are far too busy just holding things together. Asking "what do I want?" feels like a luxury. With some education, support, and acknowledgment, women like these can turn the trajectory of their lives and the well-being of their entire family. My mom is living a beautiful retirement, enjoying time with friends, rediscovering herself, and now eating the sweet fruits of her sacrifice and labor. Way to go, Mom!

WOMEN ARE FIERCE FIGHTERS

Women are persistent, adaptable, and determined. Many of the women I have met over the years have started like my mom with next to nothing at fifty and secured their retirement by their late sixties. When you get backed into a corner you come out fighting! It makes me think of the days when I worked at the wildlife center, as we often had to deal with raccoons. Those were the only animals that necessitated specialized cages.

When I needed to tend to a wound or do a hands-on examination, one volunteer would grab the two handles on the side of the cage and pull them forward as hard as possible. That would slide back of the cage forward and squeeze the raccoon against the front of the cage, immobilizing it so I could sedate it with an injection. It was called a "squeeze cage." Without sedation, that raccoon and all its flexibility and ferociousness would tear me apart (and a couple did over those years). It didn't matter that it weighed just fifteen pounds—raccoons would do severe damage to anyone within an arm's length—temporary sedation was the only way to deal with their intensity. It's a fair simile, that women can be much like these raccoons. Women are feisty and tenacious, and still adorable! Yet we are deeply protective, often fearful, and can scare easily. Women who overcome are incredible.

In my podcast, aptly named *She Handled It!*®, I've interviewed dozens of women who have faced and overcome tremendous adversity. They share their most difficult moments and how they made it through, whether those hurdles are self-imposed or completely unexpected (you can find those on my website, Apple Podcasts, Spotify, YouTube or whatever platform you listen on). It was through those shows I have confirmed there is a thread that runs through the DNA of a woman, and that's to do what is necessary to overcome. I know those stories will inspire you!

You can change your life for the better. The question is, *are you willing to do the work?* It's not enough to have a desire; you'll need to take the actual steps to learn, think, seek help, and make some changes. For example, in this book, I'm laying out a blueprint for you. I'm showing you the steps. Will you follow through? Of course you will—your favorable future depends on it!

You are remarkable! No one can care for you the way you can care for you. You are your best life plan, and that's good news.

THE GOOD NEWS

Women are fierce and determined, and we continue to permeate areas of study and lead in arenas that were once dominated by men. Finance is one of them.

Statistics women should marvel in:

- ▲ 51 percent of wealth is in the hands of women—an estimated $22 trillion worth[2].
- ▲ Nearly 13 million businesses in the U.S. are owned by women, representing 42 percent of all businesses[3].
- ▲ Women are 3 percent more likely to start a business than men[4].

---

2 https://www.newyorklifeinvestments.com/assets/documents/lit/women-and-investing/infographic-women-and-investing-part-1.pdf
3 https://www.incfile.com/blog/women-in-business-statistics#:~:text=42%25%20of%20all%20U.S.%20businesses,start%20a%20business%20than%20men.
4 https://www.incfile.com/blog/women-in-business-statistics#:~:text=42%25%20of%20all%20U.S.%20busi-

- The number of businesses owned by minority women has grown by over 163 percent since 2007[5].
- Women are responsible for between 70-80 percent of all consumer purchases[6].
- Women get better investing returns than men by nearly 1 percent. They are more disciplined and are better savers[7].
- By 2030, American women are expected to control much of the $30 trillion in financial assets that baby boomers will possess—a potential wealth transfer of such magnitude that it approaches the annual GDP of the United States[8].
- Women are graduating from college at a much faster rate than men, with both undergraduate and graduate degrees67 percent of women invest outside of retirement plans as of 2021, up from 44 percent in 2018[9].

Maybe you're reading those statistics and saying, "Well, great for those women, but I feel more like your mom at forty-three." Take heart. Current problems are always temporary. You have been created with a purpose, and it is never too late to start rewriting your story. Don't eliminate yourself. You must invest in your education because nothing will change if you don't think differently.

Albert Einstein once said: "Problems cannot be solved with the same mindset that created them." (Insanity is doing the same thing over and over, and expecting different results.)

---

nesses,start%20a%20business%20than%20men.
5 https://archive.mbda.gov/sites/mbda.gov/files/media/files/2018/2018-state-of-women-owned-businesses-report.pdf
6 Baghai, Pooneh; Howard, Olivia; Prakash, Lakshmi; Zucker, Jill. "Women as the next wave of growth in US wealth management." McKinsey Group, July 29, 2020. https://www.mckinsey.com/industries/financial-services/our-insights/women-as-the-next-wave-of-growth-in-us-wealth-management
7 Daly, Lyle. "Women and Investing: 30 Years of Research and Statistics Summarized." Motley Fool, March 1, 2023. https://www.fool.com/research/women-in-investing-research/
8 https://www.mckinsey.com/industries/financial-services/our-insights/women-as-the-next-wave-of-growth-in-us-wealth-management
9 https://www.fool.com/research/women-in-investing-research/#:~:text=gender%20pay%20gap.-,Understanding%20women%20and%20investing,quite%20a%20bit%20of%20progress.

EVERY JOURNEY STARTS WITH A SINGLE STEP

On my 47th birthday, I participated in my first ever endurance race, 29029 Everesting. The premise is you have 36 hours to hike the vertical equivalent of Mt. Everest—29,029 vertical feet. This hike was at Snowbasin Ski Resort in Huntsville, Utah in the middle of August. Once you hike up the 2,300 vertical feet of dry ski slope, you ride the gondola down. If you can repeat that ascent thirteen times in 36 hours, you have "Everested." I learned so many valuable lessons the first time I did that race, but two stand out most of all: *don't focus on how far you must go* (try to avoid future-tripping) and *just focus on the next step* (work to be fully present in the here and now).

My own mother's story has had a happy ending, but it's been no fairy tale. The journey was long, arduous, and much more difficult than it should have been. Still, no matter how tough the terrain got, she just kept taking one more step. She didn't quit on herself. Nor was she ever intimidated by the pull of freedom and the goals that she had set.

I meet many women who are hurting, scared, resentful, confused, and want to make a change. Anyone can do it, but we must do the work. It wasn't enough for me to want to make that Everest-sized climb, I had to train five to seven days a week for five months. First, I set my goal (focused my intention), then I educated myself and trained for it. I did the small things like stretching and the big things like a 10-hour hike, and everything in between. Along the way I got direction from trainers, a nutritionist, my naturopathic doctor, a sports chiropractor, massage therapists and physical therapists, and made my way forward. They all provided sage advice, but none of them could do the work for me. The effort was all mine to give or *not* give. I was going to get out what I was willing to put in. Come race day I was ready, and in 31 hours, I conquered that mountain—thirteen times—by never looking too far ahead into the distance. I took it all one step at a time (and it took me 112,284 steps to do it)!

LIVE YOUR LIFE NOW!

Today, this very moment, is all you have been promised. Don't waste it by worrying about distractions twenty years from now, or give up because of all the things that might *possibly* go wrong. Success is a pearl necklace strung from many wonderful singular pearls: do one small thing today, and add another tomorrow. Piece by piece, your brave and persistent actions will add up to something beautiful.

Once you start, keep going—and never, ever give up! We all know someone who has handled it, and we can likewise create our own incredible stories as women who made the difference. This is how we make history.

BOOKS ARE GREAT THERAPISTS

A perfect way to find guidance in a non-threatening way is reading books (such as this one). You don't have to go very far, and it's a perfectly private experience. Partner your reading with a journal, and you're setting yourself up for success. Now, take notes and carry through on what they say. Putting a cover on your book (remember doing that with a brown paper bag in high school?) will dissuade opinions or potential feelings of resentment from loved ones, so you can focus on the topics and never worry about explaining yourself to others. Or read it on an eReader. Again, if you feel the need to hide your education from your spouse, take a long and hard look at your relationship and seek help to overcome those issues (single women, aren't you glad you don't have to worry about that one?).

Stop waiting for someone else to care for you, or for your situation to magically change, and start working on yourself *now*. As you're getting into shape, you'll be better able to care of your loved ones and children. You are so very capable. Don't tell yourself you can't. Be your biggest cheerleader, not your own worst critic. It's never too late to get things in order, and there is no single situation that is beyond improvement.

If you truly feel you have waited too long to work on your finances, I recommend David Bach's phenomenal book, *Start Late Finish Rich*, for anyone who feels stuck with complacency, excuses, or fear. David offers a practical message with actionable steps to help anyone who is motivated for a better financial life after fifty. It is not too late for you.

> *"A woman is like a tea bag; you never know how strong it is until it's in hot water."* – ELEANOR ROOSEVELT

Important note: if you find yourself in a compromising or heated situation whenever you try and talk about these things with your spouse, please seek advice from a trained professional. Economic instability can be one of the major side effects of a difficult relationship, and you may be afraid of making any kind of changes for fear of rocking the boat. You may need a counselor or therapist to deal with some baggage that makes these discussions near impossible. Your partner should want the very best for you—for both of you—and not hold you back, but that doesn't mean that they are ready to face their own issues. You need to be able to learn, ask questions, assess where you are, and grow. I realize that many women may have difficulty discussing these things with their spouse, but there should never be any rules or conditions on your taking personal responsibility. If you want to better yourself, your partner should be supportive. If your desire to become educated and empowered is seen as a threat, I strongly urge seeking professional help. Put yourself first.

You can and *you will*.

Books from the library, online videos, and podcasts are free, and you can listen or read while getting ready for work or driving in your car (those resources are all at the back of this book). Don't devalue the small, seemingly insignificant seed you have in your hand right now. There is so much that is right in your world. Focus on those things.

Pay attention to your dreams. Water that small seed and know that things will get better, not just for you, but for the generations coming up behind you. If it's not enough for you to change for yourself, then think about the others who need you to charge ahead and show them what is possible.

Greatness and generosity lie within you, too.

> *You can't give to others what you do not have. You are blessed to be a blessing.*

MOST IMPORTANT TAKEAWAYS

1. Women are awesome and they are doing great things in the area of business and investing!

2. To reinvent your life, you need to think new thoughts. Get educated. Read books. Listen to podcasts. See a financial advisor (or maybe also a therapist or counselor).

3. Current problems are always temporary.

4. You need education about your finances, and you must pass that on to the next generation because your children will copy what they see. Modeling good choices will prepare your children for real life.

NEXT STEPS

1. Head to the library and check out some of the books mentioned in the resources page in the back of this book, and begin consuming new thoughts every day. Consistency is key. A supertanker doesn't change direction immediately. Slow and steady wins the race.

2. Download two to three podcasts about money (some of my top recommendations are in the resources in the back of this book). Get fanatical about learning new things and changing your life. Get comfortable with being out of your comfort zone because you will find a new life beyond the coziness of the status quo. Find speakers you connect with and let them wash over you.

3. Watch YouTube videos—there's lots of free stuff for you to fill your beautiful head with (search up any of the authors or podcast hosts mentioned as most have YouTube channels as well).

4. If anything is blocking you from having financial conversations at home with your partner, I would suggest that you talk to a counselor or pastor to help you work through those issues to help you feel confident and empowered. You may not be used to financial conversations, and these things take time.

5. Read positive books right before bed. No TV or electronics for the last sixty minutes before bed—that's just a good, healthy habit. But also, what you put in at the end of the day is proven to give your subconscious something to "think on" all night long. Make it worthwhile brain food!

CHAPTER 5

NOT SO GOOD NEWS

A Man is Not a Financial Plan

At fifteen, I thought a man would be my financial plan. Divorced at twenty-four, I learned my lesson the hard way. Unintentionally, I realized the same thing again at thirty-two. Randy is an amazing provider, a fantastic advisor, and an incredible husband, and he has done everything to support my dreams. Still, I ignorantly waited for him to take care of what I needed to do for myself. I certainly love his support, and it makes the journey a lot easier when two are yoked up and heading in the same direction—*but I am ultimately responsible for me.*

No one can expect to exist as June Cleaver, where her husband comes home, bringing the bacon, and all she has to do is vacuum the carpet while wearing lipstick and prepare a pot roast. This is the real world, where we share responsibility and decisions, and nothing comes automatically. Furthermore, life can change in an instant, and we cannot rely one hundred percent on any kind of safe domestic system to take care of us. Even if you have the most comfortable life situation—and God bless you—it's important to participate and be ready. It would be like holding your breath for the next forty years, saying "My husband is going to do the breathing for me!"

Self-care and personal responsibility belonged to me, and they belong to you. You must captain your own financial ship, even if you are coupled. At the very least, you must be a well-equipped first mate on that ship who can handle the cargo and lives under your care. It makes me so proud that you have read this far because it shows that you desire to understand more clearly what you need to do to care for your own precious life.

Pat your wonderful self on the back! You've got this!

GLARING REALITY OF IT ALL

There is so much wealth flooding into the hands of women, yet we still have a sobering reality:

- Over half of women ages 25 and older said they don't consider themselves financially secure, with 77 percent of low-income women saying the same[10].
- Women's investment account balances lag behind men's by up to 44 percent due to the gender pay gap[11].
- 41 percent of women expect to retire after age 70, if at all[12].
- 76 percent of women worry that Social Security will not be there for them when they are ready to retire[13].
- Women must plan on Social Security shortfall when retirement planning[14].

---

10 Greenberg, Gregg. "Women's fear about retirement cuts across party lines." Investment News, May 16, 2023. https://www.investmentnews.com/womens-fear-about-retirement-cuts-across-party-lines-237602.
11 Daly, Lyle. "Women and Investing: 30 Years of Research and Statistics Summarized." Motely Fool, March 1, 2023. https://www.fool.com/research/women-in-investing-research/
12 "Emerging From the COVID-19 Pandemic: Women's Health, Money, and Retirement Preparations." 22nd Annual Transamerica Retirement Survey of Workers, November 2022.
13 https://transamericainstitute.org/docs/default-source/research/emerging-from-covid-19-pandemic-women-health-money-retirement-report.pdf
14 https://finance.yahoo.com/news/workers-must-plan-on-social-security-shortfall-when-retirement-planning-advisers-say-203114970.html?

- Women often bear the financial burden of parent care[15].
- 80 percent of men die married and 80 percent of previously married women die single[16].
- Nearly half of couples don't know the passwords, or how to find the passwords, for their spouses' bank, credit card, investment, or social media accounts[17].
- 43 percent of couples don't agree on the age to retire[18].
- The average age of becoming a widow is 59[19]
- 54 percent of couples disagree on how much they need to save for retirement[20].
- Women are living, on average, seven years longer than men[21].

If you are single, be thankful that many of those statistics don't apply to you. But if marriage is somewhere on your horizon, please keep this in mind and make sure you are fully prepared with eyes wide open prior to your wedding day. If you are divorced, you likely felt the impact of some of those statistics from years gone by.

It's common knowledge that women live longer than their male counterparts, but let's put things into perspective. What was the average life expectancy for humans (male and female) in the year 1900?

The answer: Forty-seven. Can you believe that? Forty-seven! That stat makes smoke come out of my head just trying to make sense of it. Just 124 years ago, you'd have a mid-life crisis in your twenties! If you were alive, it meant that you were working. Long-term retirement,

---

15 https://www.agingcare.com/articles/daughters-care-more-for-parents-than-sons-171474.htm
16 https://www.marketwatch.com/story/this-is-something-young-married-women-should-pay-attention-to-2017-04-28
17 https://www.theladders.com/career-advice/survey-64-of-americans-know-their-partners-bank-passwords
18 https://www.kiplinger.com/retirement/601791/when-only-one-spouse-retires#:~:text=A%202018%20Fidelity%20Investment%20survey,boomers%20disagreeing%20with%20their%20partner.
19 https://www.cnbc.com/2020/03/06/recent-widows-need-financial-guidance-after-a-spouses-death.html#:~:text=I%20fit%20the%20norm.,their%20husbands%20by%2015%20years
20 https://www.foxbusiness.com/markets/43-of-couples-disagree-on-this-important-retirement-matter
21 https://www.health.harvard.edu/blog/why-men-often-die-earlier-than-women-201602199137#:~:text=In%20fact%2C%2057%25%20of%20all,about%207%20years%20longer%20worldwide.

as we know it, really didn't exist. Now people are living well into their eighties and beyond, which makes longevity the biggest risk you now face in retirement.

Not market risk. Not taxes. Not inflation—longevity. It's the risk of outliving your money.

You may need to rely on your retirement savings for thirty to forty years. I am grateful we get to have so much more time to spend with those we love, doing those things that impact others and bring us joy. But being retired for thirty to forty years brings with it a host of planning factors.

Then there are other elements that adversely affect your retirement. Women are more likely to take on the burdens of childcare, even when both parents work. Daughters often bear more of the responsibility for parent care than their brothers, which means that women will spend more time out of the workforce caring for kids or parents, compared to their male counterparts. That means that they pay less money into Social Security or a retirement savings plan and thus receive less in their retirement years.

All of these caretaker roles are a testament to how amazing and resilient women are, but they likewise take a disproportionate financial, emotional, and health toll.

JUST TELL ME I NEVER HAVE TO GO BACK TO WORK

Lily attended one of my seminars in June 2008. Soon after, she took me up on my offer for an initial visit at our office. During our meeting, I discovered that Lily had lived through many of the not-so-good life statistics that plague women across our country. Lily unofficially retired at fifty-three to care for her mom, who died four years later from complications with dementia. Lily's dad had passed away many years before. Now that Lily was in her late fifties, she didn't want to go back to work, and her husband James didn't want that either. James was sixty-two, enjoyed a great-paying job, and intended on working until Medicare kicked in at sixty-five, then he was joyfully going to retire with his bride. Their initial big plan was to explore Europe riding some of the exciting bicycle tours they had been reading about, which would give them the chance to discover some little-known towns for great wine and local cheeses.

But their passports were never stamped.

Just one month before Lily's sixtieth birthday (mere months after their thirty-fifth wedding anniversary), James passed away from a sudden heart attack. She was devastated.

Lily came to see me as she was living out the terrible reality so many women face in and approaching retirement: she was widowed with no warning. Much of her life focus had been raising their children, and then four more years looking after her ailing mother. Those life choices took her out of the labor force, which kept her from years of contributing to Social Security or a 401(k).

When she came in to see me, I wanted to shift her focus to what truly mattered—her core values—rather than the larger details of her money. Lily told me that she wanted security and independence, she did not want to have to go back to work, and she absolutely did not want to be a burden on her kids. She couldn't stand to subject her children to the same hardships she had faced while caring for her own mother over those four years.

After discussing the deep emotional impact of moving into retirement without her beloved husband, I wanted to talk through her current options, realistically. Retirement was inevitable, so how was she going to embrace it, make it happen, and enjoy it as much as possible, while honoring James's memory?

Probing a bit more, she recounted that she and her husband had often dreamed about traveling with their kids and grandkids on a big Disney Cruise on their dime—a once-in-a-lifetime trip. She also had other destinations she now wanted to explore herself, and thought she could begin to travel with some girlfriends, or her sister. Family time, personal growth, friendship, and appreciating the world—

these were the things that really mattered to her. Talking about that big family trip brought a smile to her face, and a sense of joy back into her heart.

With the way life is, there are bound to be surprises, and this is something a great planner should keep firmly in mind when planning for your retirement. You don't want to get to age sixty-five, sitting in the corner, and think, "I wish I'd done things differently." You must take care of yourself, and this is your one life—you have every right to enjoy it.

Even though all her financial pieces were going to need attention, we needed to start at the core of what money meant to her. That was the true starting line, and that is where it all began. We'll hear more about Lily's story in Chapter Seven.

SADLY, THERE'S MORE—GRAY DIVORCE

I recall one day I had six initial visits with different female clients. This day stood out because each of those women had been married at some time in their lives, and all were now divorced and single.

Somewhere between a third and a half of marriages end in divorce, depending on the source you use. It used to be the "seven-year itch," but those who have been married longer than twenty-five years are now the fastest-growing segment to get divorced. This is called "Gray Divorce," which happens over the age fifty.

- The divorce rate for people over fifty is predicted to triple by 2030[22].

- Women experienced a 45 percent decline in their standard of living (measured by an income-to-needs ratio), whereas men's dropped by just 21 percent[23].

---

22 Hughes, Ph.D., Carol R.; Fredenburg, M.S., LMFT, Bruce R. "Why the Divorce Rate for Older Couples Keeps Rising." Psychology Today, August 16, 2021. https://www.psychologytoday.com/intl/blog/home-will-never-be-the-same-again/202108/why-the-divorce-rate-older-couples-keeps-rising
23 I-Fen Lin, PhD and Susan L Brown, PhD. "The Economic Consequences of Gray Divorce for Women and Men." Journal of Gerontology Series B, Psychological Sciences and Social Sciences, December, 2021–76(10). https://www.ncbi.nlm.nih.gov/pmc/articles/PMC8599059/

While some studies have shown that men fare worse emotionally following a divorce because they tend to have fewer social connections on their own, common sense would say that women have a more difficult time, financially speaking. Since women are more likely to have dropped out of the workforce (stalling careers and putting retirement savings on hold) to care for children or aged parents, they don't see any financial recompense in a Gray Divorce for those sacrifices.

Consider that, by the time you reach retirement age, you are not the same person you were when you first married—and neither is your husband. It may be that the two of you have "grown apart," or the transition of the empty nest was quite significant. One spouse may desire great change, and might have completely different desires for retirement. However, it can also be due to money and spending habits. Financial issues during the prime earning years, if left unresolved, can overwhelm when it comes to retirement. Differences in spending habits become very clear once you are living on a fixed income budget, as does debt. The actual strain of financial worry can come between spouses, and mediation is key in situations such as these.

When I state that "a man is not a plan," I am not at all bashing men. I adore my husband and the incredible work he has done for women, men, and families over his thirty-eight-year career. We are also raising our three amazing young men to be strong, supportive, and respectful. If they decide to get married (as our oldest did this year to a stellar woman with his same first name, Morgan—yep, that happened), I want them to help care for and support their future wives, but I don't want them to be the sole key to those women's success or happiness. It's impossible to be someone's end-all-be-all. Only God is perfect. I want any future daughter-in-law to be able to adequately stand on her own, making the combined sum of her and my son much stronger than the individual parts.

"A man is not a plan" simply means this: don't make anyone else responsible for your well-being and happiness. And don't hold anyone else responsible for your unhappiness, either! If something isn't working, you have the grace and ability to fix it. You are a vivacious human creature with opinions, needs, dreams, desires, and purpose. Don't give your power away.

NO ONE SAID THIS WOULD BE EASY

Regarding Gray Divorces—making changes within the long history of a relationship is not easy. I do not want to sugar-coat this. I can likewise point to the monumental struggle that Randy and I worked through, over a span of years. At times as I lay balled-up, crying on the bathroom floor—the financial pressure of our business felt insurmountable. By putting all the financial decision-making and know-how on Randy, I had set him up for failure. But, early on in my mental awakening, when I started to claim my personal financial responsibilities, it made Randy feel as though I didn't trust him. I was upsetting the status quo.

We were able to get out of the cycle by improving our communication, seeking help, reading books, and staying true to ourselves—as a team. Let me say again: *it was difficult for many years, but so worth it.* Quitting seemed easier in the beginning, but it would have been vastly more costly in the end. The struggle and arguments are worth the understanding and connection that comes later. It is okay to want to quit—just don't.

There are sincere emotional aspects to the retirement era, and we cannot discount them in the planning process. The "Golden Years" are to be the most ideally enjoyable ones of our lives, where we finally get to do *what* we want *when* we want. But the "what" and "when" may be very different for you, compared to the desires of your spouse. Maybe his idea of a good retirement is solitude and a lakeside cabin in the country, while you want to be an active suburban grandmother with family staying over every weekend.

Do you want to tackle yearly endurance hikes like me, while your husband tinkers in the garage or rocks out on stage like Randy? Randy has no desire to hike even a small mountain with me, but he supports my desire to stretch myself physically and mentally, but it did take him a moment to warm up to the idea since he could not see the benefit or draw at first, only the time that was consumed with training. Yet he doesn't make me feel guilty because I don't get joy from digging in the dirt or riding our John Deere lawnmower. Have you talked about your wishes? Are there giant assumptions waiting to erupt, or are you even talking about retirement? It's one thing to discuss financial investments and Social Security, but these conversations need to cover what retirement will look and feel like, logistically and personally—the day to day.

A GREAT ADVISOR WILL HELP YOU SUCCEED

Communication will be the bridge to a happy compromise for whatever your retirement needs to be. It is most beneficial to work with a financial advisor during this process, because that professional will know exactly how to have these conversations, and the kind of planning that your dreams will entail. He or she will help you brainstorm and see the long-term effects, financially and emotionally.

Yet, please note: not all financial advisors are created equal.

Retirement planners are different than those that focus on growing and accumulating wealth in your twenties, thirties, and early forties. You must hire a professional that is well-versed in the financial, mental, and emotional changes that come during retirement, not just your investments and balance sheet. I will talk more about how to choose an advisor and what to look for, but know this: you need a specialist in this area, not a financial "general practitioner."

As we age, so do our circumstances. Our bodies and health situations change. As Dr. Stacy Sims, author of the health book for women, *Roar*, states, "You are not a small man, stop eating and training like one." This applies to finances too. Things change and so do our ideas of a good life, and for retirement. Change is healthy—and inevitable. But we must talk about those changes. If you are facing retirement with financial difficulties, get educated and hire a financial advisor you both like to act as your money therapist. In my own life, we had to work on the way we talked about money before we could help our actual money issues. As hard as it was to realize that I was the much of the problem, it was empowering to know that I was also much of the solution! Does any of this sound familiar to you?

Come on, Wonder Woman (or any other superhero you better connect with), you've got this handled!

IRRESPONSIBILITY AND IGNORANCE DON'T PAY YOUR BILLS

You may be placing your trust in a man, a woman, inheritance from your parents, or the government. Trust isn't bad. It's healthy to have confidence. But all those sources can let you down if you wield trust blindly. We are all broken and faulty people, and we cannot be the sole source for anyone's joy or success—nor should we place that full responsibility on someone else; that's foolish.

Let's say that you and your husband want to eat at a restaurant tonight. He asks, "Where do you want to go?" and your immediate answer is, "I don't care. Anything is fine." That's your usual answer, and it comes quite easily. But what do you really want? He shrugs and suggests a local sushi place. Whether you want sushi or not, you've already agreed to it with your passive "anything is fine" answer. What if you want a steak? What if, all week, you've been thinking about a good cheesy pasta? Speak up! He wants to hear your opinion! Otherwise, he would not have asked.

Women do this all the time. But we do it in all kinds of life decisions—not just dinner. The problem is that we don't want to hurt people's feelings or make waves. We want to take up the least amount of space possible. But that's not telling the truth! We women are notorious for subjugating ourselves and not speaking up—but this is a no-no especially when it comes to finances. Remember that your husband will most likely pass away before you, so by not having a life plan opinion, you set yourself up for failure. What happens when no one is there to make the decisions for you? If you are married, you need to do your full part!

My desires for you are to understand what you have, know where your money is, and know how to make it all function optimally. Life can change in an instant, so you need to have a clear plan. Let's make a strong one and walk this wonderful road of life together.

Are you with me?! Throw on your stilettos, cross-trainers, or hiking boots, and let's get walking!

I've heard it said that "the pain may not have been your fault, but the healing is your responsibility!" You cannot waste time putting off the action you need to take. Your financial predicament may not be your fault, but the healing of it is your responsibility.

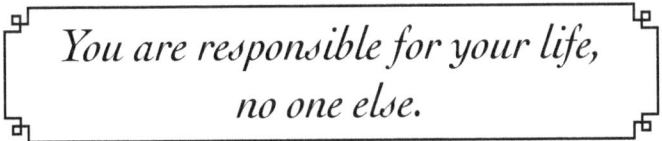

You are responsible for your life, no one else.

MOST IMPORTANT TAKEAWAYS

1. A man is not a plan—you are not a victim of your circumstances; you are a victor!

2. Longevity (outliving your money) may be the biggest risk you face in retirement.

3. Couples need to get on the same page about money and retirement by having those conversations and speaking honestly. Getting an advisor on board or a money therapist who can referee those talks. There is no right or wrong, just two different opinions.

4. You will likely be the last woman standing—80 percent of women die single.

5. Caring for parents or kids puts you "a leg down" financially.

6. Divorce often financially affects women more so than men.

7. Remember, taking responsibility means telling the truth. If you do not speak what is on your mind and say what you need to say, you are not being totally honest.

NEXT STEPS

1. Determine today that you—and no one else—are in control of your finances—YOU ARE THE PLAN. This is your one life.

2. Take your partner to a neutral place, like a coffee shop or a park, and have a candid conversation with them about financial values. Discuss what money means to you, as well as your priorities, goals, concerns, and motivations. Whatever it takes, start the dialogue. Don't let fear or differences stop you from having these discussions. Be positive, but don't worry about being right or being nice.

3. Keep reading and studying. Your education on this topic is paramount—your BEST LIFE depends on it (on you).

CHAPTER 6

YOU NEED A PLAN

> *Execution is a critical element toward becoming great.*

HE WAS THE BRAINS AND I WAS THE BRAWN

"You need to talk to your financial advisor," were the words scribbled on a piece of torn yellow legal pad paper. Betty had just arrived at our office to pick up her taxes, and handed us this ominous scrawled note. Up to this moment, we had never met Betty—only her husband, Ron. They were tax clients of the CPA who shared our office. Many couples, like Ron and Betty, have one person that handles the preparation of the return. That wasn't unusual, but Betty's situation was.

Betty contacted us, via email, about one month before April 15th to tell us her husband was ill. Just a couple of weeks later, he passed away, so she had come in that day to pick up her taxes. After the door opened, we met two women. One was Betty and the other woman was a girlfriend of hers. With her friend's help, we found out for the first time that Betty was deaf.

Betty had been married forty-six years to the love of her life. They met as teenagers. He had polio as a child. "He was the brains, and I was the brawn," she said. She meant he handled all the finances and the *thinking stuff,* and she handled all the physical labor in the house and their lives. Very quickly, it became apparent that this was one of the most financially-detached client cases I would ever see. She knew how to write a check and knew where they banked, but that was it. Betty and Ron had no children. Betty had no living siblings.

She was utterly and frighteningly alone, and extraordinarily vulnerable.

The wrinkled, yellow piece of paper was written by their attorney: *You need to talk to your financial advisor.*

She handed it to me and asked if we could help her—although she was deaf, she could respond verbally. This moment started the clock on our deep dive over the next eight weeks. We had six appointments—two more than our typical new client process, because the communication barrier obviously created a few challenges.

Randy came up with a great plan. Instead of us writing messages back and forth on her little spiral notebook, we would use the talk-to-text functions on our phones and tablets to communicate our ideas to her. Genius! But we couldn't just pick up the phone and do a conference call with her investment companies to order forms, make changes, and such. With a non-hearing client, we needed to be more resourceful and patient.

Our first visit was revealing. Betty didn't know what an IRA or brokerage account was, nor did she know if they had life insurance or if her husband had a pension. At the end of that initial meeting, we grabbed samples of different statements—life insurance, annuities, brokerage accounts, IRAs, and others—saying, "Betty, take these home and try and find something that looks like this!"

On her second visit, she brought in a stack of papers more than a foot high, some of it more than twenty-years-old, with a musty smell of aging paper and ink. We began filtering through the documents, trying to figure out what was current and if it had anything to do with their financial picture. It was tedious, investigative work, but every visit ended the same way. Betty felt relieved to have our attention and help. She would have tears in her eyes (and so would we) as she gave us giant hugs.

THE GREATEST FINANCIAL FEAR

I will never forget the day when Betty looked across the table at Randy and me and bluntly asked, "Arwen, am I going to be broke?"

She echoed the single greatest fear of most retirees, particularly common after the recession of 2008. It's gut-wrenching to discuss the panic of running out of money, but it's an unfortunate reality for many women who experience poverty after the death of their spouse. My response was very clear, assured, and simple, "Betty, you are taken care of for the rest of your life." Phew! Her husband did a great job stewarding their finances and now our role was to pull all of it together into a plan she could understand in simplified terms.

We did for her exactly what we did do for all those who sat at our table. Taking all the financial items she owned, along with pension and Social Security, we plugged them into our retirement calculator to generate a clear picture of how it might all work together (or what we might need to reposition). For Betty, as with all of our clients, we strove to leave her better than we "found her," putting her imminent worries in perspective with the bigger picture. The goal of a great planner is to show you how all the parts of your financial world fit in concert with one another. The financial advisor process is designed to provide clarity, security, and direction to be able to take the very next step.

Betty needed such clarity and direction.

Her husband had done a superb job saving for the future, but the husband-and-wife communication had been non-existent. She had no idea how to even recognize a financial document, or where things might be kept. With a little courage and some professional help, she eventually showed herself to be a financially savvy client, and we were proud of that. You should have seen her in just a few short years following his death—digging into her tax returns, asking thoughtful and educated questions, and making her own decisions; she had finally handled it!

HER STORY IS NOT UNIQUE

I look back on her story and see so many other narratives layered into her frustration. At the very least, a couple needs to communicate where important information is kept, so that the spouse, children, and beneficiaries at least know where to begin. It might be even a simple single sheet of paper where accounts, insurance, and investments are listed along with the advisor's contact information. What is the use of being prepared if you can't even locate the basic outline?

Betty was a client of ours for 10 years until her passing, but she told me very clearly, "If my story can help any other woman out there not make the same mistake, please share it!" *Miss you, Betty!*

Therefore, you need to have a clear plan that is comprehensive and easy to understand—a plan that is communicated and easily accessible. Do not delay—start now. This applies if you are married or single, because someone will need to come behind you and pick up the pieces following your death (be it a spouse, significant other, kids, or grandkids), or any other kind of event that compromises the status quo. Please make it easier on yourself and those you cherish.

TIME FOR A PLAN, BUT WHERE TO START?

Climbing 29,029 vertical feet in 31 hours, as with my *Everesting* challenge, doesn't start with a four-hour hike. It doesn't even start with a 30-minute walk! It starts by gathering the proper gear for your journey. What do you have on hand and what do you need to acquire to start your training?

Same applies for tackling your own financial mountain. We're going to begin with a little bit of inventory. Before you ignore this—I know, it's a bit of work—remember this is where real change begins! We're not going to dive too deep or be exhaustive (again, we don't start training with a 4,000-foot hike), but this baby step can make all the difference in starting on the right financial path. Worrying and feeling frustrated never changes things and will only mentally tire you out. Taking action will give you confidence and motivation.

We're going to do some basic financial accounting. Grab a pencil and begin to jot down anything you know about these items below. Dog-ear the corner of this page or bookmark it on your eReader. Write directly on this page—circle, star, or highlight anything of question—and bring it to your advisor (or take notes in the journal on your nightstand). If it doesn't apply, skip it, but if you are unsure, make a note to get some direction when you sit down with your financial advisor.

- Social Security value at full retirement age (FRA)
- Pensions: PERS, TRS, company-sponsored
- Rental income/real estate
- Individual Retirement Accounts (IRAs)
- Roth IRAs
- Brokerage accounts
- Company plans: 401(k), 403(b), 401(a), 457, TSP, etc.
- Solo 401(k), SEP-IRA, etc.

- Annuity contracts: variable, fixed, indexed, immediate
- Life insurance: whole, IUL, universal, term
- Long-term care
- Certificates of deposit
- Money markets
- Checking and savings
- Any other policies or accounts with any value

AND THE INHERITANCE GOES TO...

Our 85-year-old client, Joyce, brought in her new husband. She had been with us for several years, but after being widowed, she rekindled a relationship with a gentleman she had known over the past four decades. He didn't have a financial advisor, but after three years of marriage to our client, he liked the care and service his new bride was receiving and thus decided to meet with me to see if we could improve his situation.

Gordon spoke about his 401(k) from Boeing and a trust he had for his kids with his ex-wife. He had been divorced now for eleven years, and his priorities were leaving a legacy to his children and taking care of Joyce. As I asked more questions, I determined that he retired from Boeing in 1993, but never rolled his Boeing company plan out into an Individual Retirement Account (IRA).

"Gordon, why didn't you roll your VIP (401(k) at Boeing) into an IRA once you left?"

His response: "I didn't know I could."

This was shocking—it was hard to believe that twenty-five years had passed, and he still didn't know that he could have (or better said, *should have*) rolled his qualified retirement plan into an IRA once he left Boeing!

Here are several important components I don't want you to miss if you still have a company retirement plan at a *former* employer:

1. Turning 401(k) money into an IRA means that now have the entire world of investment options available to you (instead of the limited offerings in a company's plan), and your retirement savings will continue to grow, tax-deferred.

2. After you have left a company (aka. separated from service), you avoid the 10 percent penalty that you would incur if you withdrew or moved it before you hit the age of fifty-nine-and-one-half.

3. If you no longer work for a company, you lose much of the control you had while you were working there. The company can decide to change the provider from Vanguard to Fidelity, for example, and if similar investments aren't available, they can just liquidate the entire account and throw it into a cash account, making a "point nothing" rate of return—all without asking your permission. Some clients of ours realized they lost out on some of the best parts of the market because the new company had moved their entire account into cash.

4. Finally, an old employer does not have a financial advisor who is going to check in with you and make sure that your beneficiaries are up to date. A great advisor you hire to walk alongside you will.

So, back to the hubby of our eighty-five-year-old client. "You know, Arwen, I tried calling Boeing a month ago to do an address change, and I was on hold for thirty-five minutes. I got irritated, so I hung up."

I smiled. "I totally understand, Gordon. We speak to Boeing all the time. I mean, we talk to Boeing so much my husband wrote a book called *Retiring from Boeing!* So, I know how frustrating it can be. We would be happy to help you with your address change, but I have one question for you: who is the beneficiary on your VIP (name of Boeing's retirement plan)?"

Gasp. Gordon glanced over at Joyce and paused for what felt like an eternity.

"Oh gosh," he choked. "It's my ex-wife!"

Yikes! His ex-wife! They had been divorced for over eleven years. His kids were contingent beneficiaries, but his ex-wife would have received more than a quarter million dollars because of that *oversight*.

This happens more times than you would think.

TRANSFER YOUR OLD COMPANY PLAN TO AN IRA

So, in summary, if have a 401(k), 403(b), TSP, or some type of retirement plan, and you no longer work for that company, you have the option to transition that money into a self-directed individual retirement account (an IRA). This is the most prudent way to control the retirement money you have earned and keep your beneficiaries up to date. This is allowed under the IRS code, so it is not a taxable event if you do it correctly. Doing it wrong can lead to painful penalties, so you want to make sure you are getting help to do it right. There are also significant benefits from consolidation, simplification, and future tax planning and reporting.

Moreover, employer-sponsored plans like 401(k)s are required to withhold a mandatory 20 percent tax on distributions (what you pull out), often more than you need to cover the tax bill. Additionally, it complicates matters when you need to start taking your Required Minimum Distributions (Chapter Nine), putting greater responsibility (and chance of making a mistake) on you.

People often forget to update beneficiaries with new spouses or grand kids, just like Gordon. Knowing what you have and who's listed as a beneficiary is vitally important to those you love and care for. For instance, we had some clients of ours call us one day to tell us their only son (and beneficiary) had passed away unexpectedly. With this information, we were able to put our team on immediate notice to gather the necessary paperwork for an appointment where we would be able to discuss the next steps with our clients. While our clients were grieving, we were ready and able to take care of their financial changes. It was a conversation that needed to happen, for the sake of our client's peace of mind and getting the current financial plan up to date. Without a proper beneficiary, what good is preparation?

This is a vitally important component to why you need a strong relationship with a financial advisor. It must be someone you can call when things are painful or confusing, so that you can depend on them to think clearly and help protect your best interests. They can help to significantly take the pressure off you, pulling together paperwork and scheduling appointments to get things moving in the right direction. Meanwhile, you will have the time and space you need to grieve and do what you need to do, not worrying about the details. They may help you avoid making big financial decisions or changes at a vulnerable time in your life.

NO MICRO-CLIMATES

So, now you have begun to organize yourself (hopefully on paper, not just in your head) and have a clear idea of what you own. You've identified what matters most to you—your values. You are thinking plainly about all the items that make up your financial life. But the perplexing question you most likely have is: "How do all these financial pieces work together to pay the bills for the rest of my life, allow me to afford future healthcare, and let me have fun, too?"

The issue that plagues a lot of women is that they unintentionally plan within *micro-climates*.

Now, the common definition of *climate* is the long-term patterns and conditions within a specific area, or the usual circumstances. It is your general environment, and the factors that keep it in balance.

A micro-climate is a small section within a larger climate that has different elements or special features.

My zoology background brings me to this analogy. The world over, you have large continents that may contain many micro-climates such as the temperate climate, polar climate, tundra, tropics, desert, etc. Each seems relatively self-contained, and the specific plants and animals that thrive in each micro-climate have different needs—if you pull an animal from the tundra and put them in the desert, the result is often death. You simply aren't going to see kangaroos and polar bears at the same party. Yet, each micro-climate blends into another until it becomes that new climate; there is always a crossover, and this is what we need to understand. They are not separate unto themselves.

As it relates to our financial world, we need to avoid doing all our planning within each micro-climate. We simply cannot put everything into perfect separate boxes, and make our decisions according to different weather patterns. On the contrary, it's a mistake to make sweeping money decisions within micro-climates. It's also incredibly stressful and wasteful of our precious time and resources. We have to think of every single thing within the larger climate picture (your entire financial world).

If you want to determine the options for your Social Security, you might reluctantly march into the Social Security office, get that information, and decide on the matter. Then you talk to your CPA or accountant about your tax issues and make plans accordingly. Next, you speak to the pension provider regarding how you should take your pension and what sounds best, and you make an irrevocable decision. Then you talk to somebody about your healthcare or long-term care needs, followed by Medicare. Following that, you speak with your broker about your at-risk assets in your investment account.

That's a lot of work.

Those are all micro-climates. You're treating them as though they function completely independent of one another.

Yet, as anyone in life sciences can explain, micro-climates must operate in compliment to each other, or the whole system falls out of balance. There must be symbiosis. Your retirement is like the whole-earth view—massive pollution in one area may cause foul weather in another. If you spend money on one thing, you may need to budget tighter on another. Your healthcare directly affects your retirement planning, and your house payments will likely depend on your investments. Overall, if you don't have a strategy for how your big picture will act in a Great-Recession-like event, then even the very best planning in each separate area may not be sufficient—at best.

Micro-climate mentality is one of the most common issues we see with individuals and couples at the start of the planning process. They try to plan each area separately, one after the other. They may have made huge, sometimes irrevocable, decisions within these micro-climates instead of making their decisions based on an inclusive and comprehensive plan that has all regions considered. This again is one of the benefits of an all-encompassing financial plan that is organized with the help of a trusted advisor. It's incredible when you see how each piece of your financial puzzle functions, separately AND collectively, and determine how it works optimally within the bigger picture. How else will you figure out when to begin Social Security or pension payments, or on what date you can confidently retire once and for all?

IT'S NOT THE BATHROOM OR THE ESCALATOR

Let's say you've arrived at the mall. There are a few shops you want to visit, but your first stop is Pottery Barn. You scan the directory, find the home furnishing category, follow your pointer finger down ah ha, Pottery Barn: 242. You turn your gaze back to the layout of the mall in front of you, first level, second, level—finally locating Pottery Barn. Found it!

Now you're on your way!

Or are you?

To determine how to get there, you must first locate the red dot indicating *YOU ARE HERE.*

This baseline plan, or *YOU ARE HERE* initial scenario, is the essential step one of planning your desired destination. You can't estimate how much money or coverage you might have in the future without knowing what you currently have and where you are *right now.*

It wouldn't be prudent to go into an appointment with a new doctor and begin with a list of the prescriptions you want them to write before they have completed a basic exam. If a doctor didn't perform a thorough assessment to determine your baseline medical condition (and ask about medications and allergies and review prior medical records), he or she could lose their license by prescribing something that could harm you. That's malpractice.

THERE'S A DIFFERENCE BETWEEN INVESTMENTS AND PLANNING

Many years back, we bought another financial professional's business. He wasn't a fiduciary—meaning a professional who is required to operate in his clients' best interests—he was just an insurance agent. His business offered only life insurance, long-term care insurance, and annuities. This isn't to say he was acting poorly, just to explain that he had a limited range of investment tools to use with his clients. His practice was truly transactional.

We began the giant process of meeting with all three hundred of his clients and building out their retirement plans (which none of them had since he was an insurance agent, not a financial planner). Day after day, we sat with each of his former clients to explain how everything they owned with him (and outside of their work with him) worked together and built them a holistic plan. For many of these clients, it was the first time they had an opportunity to visualize their full financial landscape in entirety, rather than just one policy at a time.

Some of them felt very frustrated once they realized just how many similar investments they owned. Many had policies they just didn't need, yet they were paying sizable fees for some things that didn't benefit them. The fault wasn't the products. We regularly used these same tools in many of our clients' plans. What was problematic was how the tools were applied, and to whom. Insurance and financial products must be combined and timed—otherwise, they risk being ineffective or made redundant (and just plain expensive). It would be like wearing nylon and polyester ski pants on a July afternoon in Miami, Florida—it's just not going to work in your best interest. You may need to wear pants that day, but ski pants are not the same as linen ones. Ski pants have their appropriate place, but they don't belong on a white sand beach at 72 degrees.

The same principle for physicians and doctors can be applied for giving professional financial and retirement advice. Telling you how to invest your current 401(k), what stocks you should buy, or when to take your pension or Social Security could be dangerously irresponsible if you're not looking at all the parts of your financial life and how they could be affected by these decisions.

If you're working with someone who is planning in a microclimate, they may be duplicating investments you already have or neglecting an area where you need more coverage. Additionally, an advisor wouldn't be acting in their fiduciary capacity and doing what is in your best interest, if they gave you advice without having enough information. Every investment must have a purpose and be prescribed at the appropriate time, in the proper dosage for your unique situation.

A comprehensive approach is vital to your overall financial health and longevity.

When starting out with any new advisor, you need to create a baseline for where you are and where you want to go. Knowing where you are helps build the conversation for understanding what your needs are and the timeline to work with. Your initial appointment should determine the *YOU ARE HERE* baseline. Then, once that has been established, you can run possible scenarios and see how your current plan defends against a recession, plan a mortgage payoff, or figure out a travel budget for the next ten years.

It is critical to identify where in the world you are. You don't want to make any changes to your current picture until you know exactly where you stand, *today*.

Don't make decisions based on the partial view of your current picture. No micro-climates, My Wonderful Friend—and be sure to complete the checklist earlier in this chapter to help get you started.

In these pages, I share some incredible true stories about women facing myriad financial situations. You may be going through something similar. The foundational question always remains, "Am I going to be okay?" No matter how hard your situation, how unbearable the elements, how painful the emotions, or how hopeful the potential—remember that having a trustworthy financial advisor is the common theme of how all these women came through their dark hour. You want to have that person in your corner and on your side, so that, no matter what life brings, you will have all resources in place.

> *It takes faith to believe in something better, yet you must put in the work. One can't exist without the other.*

MOST IMPORTANT TAKEAWAYS

1. Do not delay in taking inventory of what you have. Locate your financial *YOU ARE HERE*.

2. When you no longer work for a company (separate from service), you may want to consider rolling your company plan into an Individual Retirement Account (IRA) to keep greater control over your money and investment choices.

3. Make sure your beneficiaries and your mailing address stay up to date—and this is something your financial advisor should help you with. This is part of the relationship.

4. Avoid micro-climates within your financial world. Everything is related and crosses over!

NEXT STEPS

1. Complete the basic inventory questions in this chapter before moving to the next chapter.

2. If you no longer work for a company, and you still have money there in a company plan of some kind, get help from an advisor to consider opening an IRA and roll it over to retain greater control of your assets. You can combine multiple old company plans into one IRA. No need for multiple IRAs.

3. Meet with a fiduciary (looking out for your best interests) retirement planner who has the tools to help you combine all that you own in a single picture in order to help you make the right decisions about your money and future. Start interviewing individuals within the next six weeks. Don't let momentum get away, and meet with two or three (or more) to find a great

fit. Your self-imposed deadline to have a first meeting with someone: ___/___/___.

4. When you find an advisor that you feel confident speaking to, allow him or her to process your information and give you an initial *YOU ARE HERE* projected plan. The initial appointment should not come with a fee, as they are there to get to know you and understand how they might be of service. Let them explain how the process will proceed, and how they will work with you. Do you like their style? Are they clear in communication? Does the plan make sense to you? Are all your details there? What does your intuition tell you? This will give you a better idea of whom you truly want to work with. It costs nothing to have insightful first conversations with these professionals.

5. Double check your beneficiaries! This goes for insurance, investments, your company investments, and your entire current plan. Make sure you know what is going to who—and why!

CHAPTER 7

INCOME FOR LIFE

> *It's always easier to go quietly than to put up a fight. You were never built for easy.*

LET'S MAKE A DEAL!

"These people, dressed as they are, come from all over the United States to make deals at the Marketplace of America! Let's Make a Deal! And here is TV's top big dealer, Monty Hall!" (Clapping).

I loved that show as a little girl. They'd call Sally, who was dressed as a clown, a bumblebee, or a cowgirl, and she would jump out of her chair. Arms flailing, she'd land beside Monty and side-hug him, hopping up and down as he made small talk. I often imagine a Monty-Hall-style game show for the newly retired.

"Welcome, Sally, where are you from?"

In a slight southern drawl: "Well, Monty, I am originally from Savannah, Georgia, but now I live near my grandkids in Boise, Idaho!" she responds in an overly-excited voice.

"That's great! So, you love being with your grand kids?"

"More than anything! And when I retire from nursing next year, I will get to be with them more often!" she exclaims.

"Well, that's great! Okay, let's see what possible retirement options might lie behind door number one, two, or three."

The announcer's voice booms over the speakers and begins to describe the magnificent options that potentially wait behind two of those doors.

"Well Sally, behind one of these doors lies a retirement full of dreams, vacations, no money worries, and memory upon memory with your grand kids. It is full of peace, security, and life! You will never have to worry about being a burden on your kids, or having enough money if you need nursing home coverage—AND you will have the opportunity to leave money to all six of your grand kids and your three children!"

"Ooh!" The crowd responds with applause as Sally looks excitedly at the host and smiles at the audience. "Or, maybe you get a new motor home!" The crowd erupts as a brand new, class A, thirty-six-foot motor home is revealed (fully loaded with four slide-outs), valued at over $300,000.

That leaves the final option: *the booby prize.*

"All right, Sally, which door do you choose? Door number one, door number two, or door number three?" The crowd begins to shout which door they think hides the best option.

"I really want that secure and peaceful retirement. I am going to pick door number three."

"All right, please reveal what is behind door number three!"

After a long, nerve-wracking pause from the announcer: "It's a brand-new motor home!" The crowd erupts in a roar as Sally jumps up and down, then clearly begins to struggle over whether she takes the motor home or risks getting the booby prize.

"Well, Monty," she replies, "I really love that motor home, but, being a widow, I really can't see myself doing that kind of travel alone, and that's a lot to take care of for one person. So I am going to take my chance to see what is behind door number one!"

Monty smiles. "All right, Sally. So, you give up the $300,000 motor home for the hope of a peaceful retirement. Let's see—did you win that? Reveal what is behind door number one!"

As the door opens, there is enormous piggy bank with a check for $750,000 on the table. A large sign above it reads: "BROKE AT 85." Sally hears the dreaded sound of failure. "Womp-womp-wommmp." The crowd seems confused as to why that is the booby prize, and we see the same from Sally.

"Ooooh, I am so sorry, Sally, but let's see what is behind door number two." The door slides open, revealing the same piggy bank with only $250,000 in it, but the sign above it reads, "PEACEFUL RETIREMENT, $1.1 MILLION AT NINETY."

Huh? How could that be? If she starts out with three times more money, how could she be broke at eighty-five, yet have $1 million if she retires with only $250,000?

SIMPLE MATHEMATICS

People often turn to their friends, commercials, or internet articles for information about the amount of money needed for retirement. Yes, the amount is a vital consideration, but it is not the most important part of planning.

The two most essential components of retirement planning are *income* and *expenses*. Period. It's all about cash flow!

I had back-to-back visits one day that felt very much like the scenario I've outlined for our fictitious Sally. One couple came in who, when they were each sixty-five, planned to retire from jobs at a local hospital. They were both registered nurses who had put in seventy-five years, collectively, and were retiring with $250,000 saved in their retirement plans. They each had healthy pensions and Social Security benefits. They were entirely debt free and owned (free and clear) a three-bedroom, two-bath home worth $450,000, so their monthly living expenses were about $4,500 per month.

In contrast, the other couple was a similar age but had $2 million in retirement savings and no pensions. They each had Social Security benefits, yet owned a $1.9 million home with a $400,000 mortgage and a lifestyle that cost them $11,000 per month.

	COUPLE #1 - $250K IN RET.	COUPLE #2 - $2M IN RET.
Social Security (His)	$2,550	$2,550
Social Security (Hers)	$2,550	$1,800
Pension (His)	$3,100	0
Pension (Hers)	$3,300	0
Monthly Expenses	$4,500	$11,000
Money needed from Ret. Accts. (after removing 20% taxes from income)	Monthly cash flow NONE - had +$4,700 extra every month	Monthly cash flow -$7,520
Money at age 90	$1.5 million	Broke at 85

Make sense? It's simple mathematics.

Women routinely make assumptions on how much they will need in order to retire. It's common to believe that you need more than $250,000 or $500,000 to live well, and the media messaging supports that myth. We see that blown out of the water all the time. I have seen women who have started over at fifty after a divorce. In this scenario, she may come in with only $100,000 in retirement savings in her late sixties, but she has done many other things right. She keeps expenses low, is mortgage-free, maybe enjoys some rental income (or a paying roommate), or works for a government, school, or hospital, where pensions still exist. Rest assured that she is on a path to a beautiful, restful, relaxing retirement.

It's all about income overlaid with expenses—not just how much money you have, but how you use it.

For proper planning, you need to be able to see everything you have integrated into a comprehensive plan. Don't be fooled by the "big number" of retirement savings you think you need. It's crucial that you have a complete income plan that demonstrates how much money you need—month after month, year after year. Get the facts, so that you don't have to live on the false promise of good intentions.

Recall that 80 percent of married men die married, so if you are married now, the likelihood is high that your spouse may die before you both truly see the plan unfold. Yet 73 percent of couples disagree as to whether they have a retirement income plan created.

This bears repeating—*73 percent disagree*[24].

It's black or white: you either have an income plan or you don't.

Handling this money piece is imperative to your future of peace and certainty. You need an understandable document that shows how much money you need, month after month, year after year, and what your income gap could be.

MIND THE GAP

In 2016, Randy and I co-wrote a Forbes article called "Mind the Gap—In Retirement[25]." When you ride the Tube in London (public transit railway), there are signs all over that say, "Mind the Gap," referring to the gap between the platform and the train. We often use that expression for this part of retirement planning. If your monthly income is $1,200 short (income gap), then you must focus your energy to "Mind the Gap" about what you're going to do to make sure that you have $1,200 coming in from your retirement accounts.

---

[24] Richard Day Research. "2011 Fidelity Investments Couples Retirement Study." Fidelity Investments, May, 2011. https://www.businesswire.com/news/home/20110629005966/en/Fidelity-Couples-Study-Finds-Husbands-and-Wives-Not-Having-Critical-Conversations-Needed-to-Achieve-Retirement-Goals

[25] https://medium.com/@RandyBeckerFinancial/mind-the-gap-in-retirement-3df2b4ab2a0

During working years, you focus on your job, saving, raising children, volunteering, and just doing life. In the background, you accumulate a retirement nest egg—often on autopilot. You contribute a piece of each paycheck to your 401(k) and IRAs without giving it much thought until you near retirement age. The fact of the matter is, when you reach retirement, all that background work immediately comes to the foreground. It's sort of staring you square in your face, taunting you, like Goliath, ready to fight.

You can't help but look at your retirement account and say, "Well, I guess this is it. This is what I have to last for the rest of my life." Psychologically, that's a big shift for women. Still, if you don't get the *money part* out of the way, then you could spend most of your precious time trying to figure out how to beat an opponent far bigger and more formidable than you. The money giant looms large to defeat you, and you will be stepping into the fight with just a few small stones and a homemade slingshot. Yikes.

I hope you have major guts and God on your side.

In my experience, this is the main challenge that most women face—income planning. It is a massive undertaking for the untrained. How do you transition from the working years (with money coming in month after month) to suddenly *not working?* There's a significant drop in earned income. Maybe you haven't started Social Security, either. Maybe you're like most of us and not fortunate to have a pension.

Or maybe you are prepared and just don't know it yet. Your opponent may be bigger, but they are slow and sluggish. With some great coaching and direction, nimble movements, and faith, you can make Goliath fall. After all, he's big, but he has a weak spot. Women do this all the time. You can do this!

So, where do you get the income from? Let's look at some of your income options.

INHERITANCE

You head to the Midwest to celebrate Christmas with your mom. She's now in her eighties. You dispense with hugs at the door and then ask, "Mom, how are you feeling?" She responds with a spring in her step, "Great, Honey. Thanks for asking!" Perhaps you feel a twinge of disappointment.

That's not good. Really, not good at all.

My dad's mom, my nana, lived her life with the expectation of inheriting most of my great-grandfather's money. She was his only child and aside from her years of raising my dad and his three siblings, she never worked a job. Even after she and my grandfather divorced when the last kid was finally out of the house, she relied on her father to cover her financially. He was a multi-millionaire that owned the Yakima Herald newspaper. He had built (along with the effort of his dad) quite an empire. Yet my nana was unprepared for his new wife, who came into the picture in the last ten years of his eighty-six-year life.

That new woman was persuasive, and within five years following my great-grandfather's death, all the millions created by him, and his dad, were eliminated from the family line. Eighty years of wealth, gone. My nana lived much of her final decades angry, upset, and crying victim because her dad left most of his money to another woman, not her. She struggled financially in her later years yet refused to do her part and handle it. You don't want to be the kind of grandmother who leaves a legacy of bitterness to her grandchildren. We want to bring warmth, joy, and gratitude.

An estimated $30 trillion will be passed via inheritance over the next twenty years from Baby Boomers to their kids. Some of that may fall your way, but you need to have a plan that functions without that expectation. Don't make the same mistake my nana did.

THE OTHER GUYS

"What sources of income do you have?" This is a question we would ask a prospective client right away, in an initial meeting. These conversations are fundamental to all future planning.

We commonly heard the following answers: 1) part-time wages, 2) social security, 3) pension, and 4) rental income. You may be asking: what about RMDs, my annuity payments, or dividends from my investment accounts? Those are the retirement assets that help bridge the gap, and we'll dive into them in Chapter Nine. However, they are not sources of income as it relates to the income planning discussion we are currently having. This is one of the very first things you will need to share with any financial advisor you meet with.

PART-TIME WAGES

Part-time Wages: One gal worked twenty-two years for Microsoft; when she came in for her second visit, she had been unexpectedly fired. Her paycheck from Microsoft was a huge part of the planning process and was instantly eliminated. She said, "If I can stay retired, let's do it, but if I need to go back to work for a few years to make the retirement picture pristine, please let me know." At fifty-five, the retirement plan would barely sustain her though her nineties and left a lot of *what-ifs* without solid coverage. Thus, being fully retired was not her best option.

I emphasize the importance of creating a financial plan that is built out to the age of 100—especially for females. With life expectancies trending longer and medical care vastly improving (recall that life expectancy in the year 1900 was forty-nine—things have certainly changed), the best-case scenario is to plan conservatively to cover for any potential market or life surprises. You may scoff at the idea of 100 years, but think realistically: *do you want to run out of funds at the age of ninety-five?* And if that does happen, who will be around to fill in the gaps and take care of you?

Going through the intricate details of her plan, it was apparent she needed to get a job. So, she followed her passion as a photographer, setting up gigs and generating money doing what she loved.

She thought outside of the box and handled it.

> **WHY PLAN TO 100?**
>
> Centenarians are one of the fastest-growing age groups in the world. There were 89,739 centenarians living in the United States in 2021, nearly twice as many as there were 20 years ago, according to data from the Population Division of the United Nations[26]. With those sorts of statistics, even though our grandparents and parents may have only lived to their seventies or eighties, we think we it's important to prepare to be some of those who live to three digits. If you plan to live that long and don't, you may end up leaving an inheritance for your loved ones. But if you don't plan to live that long and you do, it could drastically disrupt your lifestyle, security, and peace of mind. So, particularly for women, who regularly live longer, a retirement plan should be built to last to 100.

Women, it is vital that your financial advisor builds out your plan to age 100. Trust me on this—it's far better to be safe than sorry. If you run out of funding in the very last years of life you are going to be very sorry!

SOCIAL SECURITY

And please *do not* make the mistake of thinking that Social Security will cover your income gap. Social Security started in 1935 to care for

---

[26] The United Nations, Population Division: Department of Economic and Social Affairs. "World Population Prospects 2022, Online Edition." https://population.un.org/wpp/Download/Standard/Population/

the aging population and was viewed as an entitlement of sorts, so it was not taxed. Upon its creation, Social Security turned on at age sixty-five. That was when you started receiving your benefits. What is crazy, though, is life expectancy for people in 1935 was sixty-two years! That's why retirement income planning is imperative, because Social Security probably won't be enough to meet your needs once you stop working.

There are a lot of generic concerns about Social Security, and many people are simply intimidated by the amount of paperwork involved. There are decisions to make, and without proper knowledge and guidance, those decisions can feel onerous. We also have large-scale fears that the program will not be around much longer, because of a constant ghost script that whispers that politicians are cutting budgets and pulling strings. But remember that Social Security is one of the fundamental economic and social strengths to the backbone of this country and our retirees. It is central to our entire system, just as retirement and working hard is cardinal to our American Dream.

I acknowledge the worry that Social Security might be going away, and it's important to ask those questions. As advisors, we create financial plans based on facts and utilize the tools we have available *right now*. From all available current information, we know that the Social Security program is not going anywhere, and that it will be around for the foreseeable future. Depending on government decisions, the numbers might change, but our national care-taking social system will, in the years to come, still be there. It might be a slow reduction of benefits over time, or taxes might rise, but it will be there. It's set for those who are most vulnerable in our society, and they need that money to be there. It would be absolute chaos and calamity if it was on the table to be removed.

Upon its creation, Social Security was 100 percent non-taxable, and they said it would never be taxed. Time progressed, and because people were living longer and still collecting at the same age, the government had to make changes to adapt the system. Thus, they added a tax. Then, they raised that tax: Social Security can now be taxed up to 85 percent. It is what it is. Being upset about it doesn't change anything, you just need to know how to best work in the system as it currently stands.

Here are some of the basics you ought to know about Social Security:

- Social Security has thousands of core rules, including numerous complex formulas for couples

- Social Security does not send out benefit statements any longer (if you are under the age of 60). You need to go to www.ssa.gov and create a 'My SSA' account to print out your benefit statement

- Social Security should amount to around 40 percent of your entire retirement income, but no more than 40 percent of what you will need. Plan accordingly. Your retirement picture will need to account for the remaining 60 percent, and how you use it.

- Claiming Social Security too early could cost you more than $100,000 of lifetime benefits. Retirees will lose an average of $111,000 in income per household because they took Social Security benefits too early into their retirement, rather than draw down on their own savings first. Overall, only 4 percent of retirees take Social Security at the financially optimal age, which, for 83.4 percent of them, was age sixty-seven or older. The best age depends on a host of factors, including life expectancy, other income sources, future costs in retirement and if you're married or still working[27].

---

27 Herron, Janna. "Doing this one thing with your Social Security could mean losing $100,000 in retirement." USA Today Money. https://www.usatoday.com/story/money/2019/06/28/social-security-claim-too-early-and-lose-100-000-retirement/1572620001/

▲ If you are currently divorced (and you haven't remarried) and you were married more than ten years, you have the option to collect against your ex-spouse's benefits. There are multiple rules behind this, but this is a planning option you don't want to ignore.

NOW OR LATER

Social Security is an area in which I see a lot of people planning in a micro-climate. Many of the individuals I meet with say, "I'm going to delay my Social Security, because it's more money." Or they tell me, "I got laid off from my job at sixty-two. I am going to collect early." Don't rush into either of those choices, because the decision is relatively irrevocable: if you change your mind, you can pay it all back within the first twelve months, but otherwise when that choice is made, it's made. The question should be: *what is the best choice in the context of my entire plan and for the rest of my life?*

The front page of your Social Security benefits form has a value, and that value is your full retirement age (FRA). For the women nearing or in retirement, FRA is going to be somewhere between sixty-six and sixty-seven. This figure represents 100 percent of your FRA value. Every year you delay that benefit, up to age seventy, your benefit increases by another 8 percent. That would mean at age seventy your benefit could exceed your FRA amount by 32 percent.

A lot of people automatically delay so they can receive the larger benefit. There isn't anything inherently wrong with that thought process. However, that is not always the best decision in the long term. Sometimes there are health issues that make taking Social Security earlier a better choice. Or, maybe you get laid off from work at sixty-three and can't wait for that additional income to turn on at seventy.

Or sometimes—and I love this—we look at Social Security within the context of a healthy retirement plan, and we can actually talk about taking Social Security early. Your plan doesn't rely on Social Security to function optimally. Imagine if you received an extra $2,550 every single month for the next four years, because you took Social Security at sixty-six instead of seventy? I bet you could figure out something fun to do with it!

It could help you afford something truly fulfilling—something that makes others' lives better. That money might allow you to travel more, take the grandkids somewhere cool, fly first class every now and then, or you might just want to give it away. How sweet would that be! Anything is more fun than just allowing the government to hang on to it for no specific reason.

People don't know what they don't know. Therefore, having your financial advisor run a Social Security optimization calculation for you is imperative. If your advisor doesn't do that, doesn't have access to the necessary Social Security planning tools, or just doesn't think it is important, you need to find a different advisor—immediately. Hanging on to an unfulfilling advisor relationship could possibly cost you $100,000 of your future Social Security benefits.

BRING YOUR PATIENCE

It's necessary to know all your possible options from the Social Security Administration, so make it a priority to go in and discover all the choices you have. Take a great book or headphones (so that you can listen to music or a podcast) and a large dose of patience for the wait, and don't leave until you get the facts you need to make a wise decision. This is really the best way to determine your options.

One Social Security office administrator told a client of mine that they didn't know anything about collecting benefits on an ex-husband's Social Security. That bad information from a new and uneducated Social Security employee cost the woman $1,500 per month for two years. That's $36,000! I told her to march back in there and get her benefit, to handle it. She did. But of course, Social Security won't be compensating for missed back pay for that mistake, so it's important to get all the data and talk it over with your retirement planner.

If you have heard information from trusted outside sources and are not getting the same information from the clerk at the Social Security Administration (SSA), ask for someone else and dig a bit further. Get a second opinion and further confirmation. Get a third opinion, if need be.

PENSIONS

Pensions, as we now know, are going the way of the Dodo bird. Extinct.

Most private companies no longer offer them, and those that still do are in danger of defaulting on their obligations (after decades of underfunding those investments). Pensions are expensive to maintain, cut into the "almighty profits," and reflect long-term liabilities on a company's balance sheet. Employees don't stay on the payroll for decades like they used to, so companies are more freely disposable with how they help plan for retirement—if at all.

With pensions vanishing, the responsibility of generating guaranteed lifetime income managed by professionals with decades of experience has been transferred to you, the individual, with your 401(k), 403(b), TSP, and SEP-IRA assets, and all that financial training of yours (ha ha ha).

"Joe, do you have any survivor benefits on your $3,500 pension from Hanford?"

Joe looked at me, puzzled. "What do you mean?"

"Well," I responded, "if you were to die tomorrow, how much money would Cathy receive from Hanford for the rest of *her* life?"

There was a very long pause. He glanced down at his wringing hands on the table, then back across at me.

"Nothing."

You could see the distress on his face; he and Cathy had clearly never had the matter posed to them that way.

"Why is that?" I inquired of them both. After a moment of silence, they looked at each other and then back at me.

"We just thought it was best to pick the largest amount. No one gave us any reason to do otherwise."

The biggest number isn't always the best number.

If this sixty-five-year-old man, who was married to a healthy sixty-old triathlete, were to die unexpectedly or prematurely, that $3,500 of monthly pension income would be eliminated instantly. She could easily outlive him by fifteen to twenty years. They were debt-free, and their monthly expenses totaled about $4,000, which is a very reasonable lifestyle for where they lived in the Tri-Cities area of Washington State. The pension currently met 85 percent of their income need, and on his death, that plus the smaller of the couples' Social Security benefits would be eliminated.

In dollars and cents, combining his pension and the lost Social Security (upon death of a spouse, the smallest social security is eliminated; that was hers at $1,800 per month), his death would mean a loss of $5,300 per month for his wife. She realized that 100 percent of her newly created "income gap" would be pulled from whatever retirement assets they had saved. It would be her prayer that between those assets and the remaining $2,700 in Social Security, she would have enough to survive for possibly another twenty plus years.

Thankfully Joe's pension dispersal wasn't disastrous. Cathy would have still been able to handle it financially, yet it was a very unnecessary gamble.

We see individuals and couples making this mistake all the time. They determine their pension payout in a micro-climate, speaking about only a small portion of their retirement plan to the pension provider and making vital, life-long decisions that are often irrevocable. The couple should have known first how that decision would affect the entire picture that spans both their lifetimes, not just what gave them the biggest number *right now*.

This is not to say that this couple, or others like them, was irresponsible. Quite often, it's the contrary. But without proper advice from a retirement planner who understands the bigger-picture retirement planning process, people can make disastrous choices. Before you decide, you need to understand the potential outcomes, and how the plan will perform in all circumstances, over the course of your lifetime.

We looked at all the possible *what-if* scenarios. What if they went through the worst ten years in stock market history, like 2000 through 2009? What if he died in the next decade? What if he needed some form of nursing home care and drained a large portion of their assets, and then died, eliminating the pension and the smaller of the two Social Security checks? How would all these unknowns affect her or him?

You must play this game of *what-if prior* to making decisions on collecting your pension. That is always the most effective way to make the best choice.

RENTAL INCOME

"My mom continually says to me, 'Honey, you're always broke.'" This was a statement coming from a sixty-two-year-old woman who owned six rental houses. This gal loved her rentals, enjoyed tinkering on them, and maintained a steady cash flow from their management. On many occasions, however, one or two rentals were empty for a period. As a result, income fell short, and she found herself strapped for cash. She wanted to keep trying, but her eighty-five-year-old mother saw the situation as it really was.

She was house-rich and cash-poor.

It was a simple fix: sell one of the rentals, pour that $300,000 into her retirement and POOF, no more cash-flow issues. Yet her emotional attachment to the rentals prevented her from having that peace of mind. She refused to take that advice and was instead living a life of *barely getting by*.

It's not uncommon for people to own rentals. For those who do, rentals can be a great source of income throughout retirement. We have, however, seen that those entering their seventies are focused more on simplification and consolidation than they were in their sixties. They often consider selling some or all rentals to end the frustration that comes from owning rental homes and the problems associated with tenants.

Rental management is not something most people plan on doing for life. House-rich and cash-poor doesn't put food on the table, or clothes on your back. It sure doesn't help you sleep well at night, either. Be willing to detach yourself from that asset if the time is right, and see how it will realistically affect your retirement plan. The process of selling a rental is vitally important to see in the context of the entire picture. You need to know where you currently stand, and then build out another retirement scenario that shows the elimination of the rental income (and its expenses). Don't forget to incorporate the influx of cash into your overall picture.

Additionally, you don't want to leave a legacy that maddens your heirs instead of blessing them. Many of our clients have truly enjoyed owning rentals and have benefited from them in retirement, but often their kids do not want to take over the management. You want to be able to spend confidently in retirement, so please be open to the best options for you *and* your heirs.

I KNOW WHAT I HAVE, NOW WHAT?

This is a daunting task for most individuals—how do I span that income gap, month after month and year after year? If your monthly income is $1,200 short, then focus your energy on what you're going to do to make sure you have $1,200 coming in from your retirement accounts.

I believe there are two main approaches to taking income in retirement:

THE UNCERTAIN WAY

Your first option is to simply keep the money in investment accounts that have variable returns (they go up and down with the fluctuations of the stock market), take distributions, hold on like mad, and hope for the best.

In my opinion, relying on investments that fluctuate in value to pay most of your bills in retirement is the last thing you want to do. This approach results in uncertainty and carries an ever-looming possibility of running out of money.

DOLLAR COST AVERAGING (DCA)

When you were working, you probably employed a popular strategy called dollar-cost averaging, or DCA. The fancy definition of DCA is: an investment strategy that aims to reduce the impact of volatility on purchases of financial assets (for example, equities and stocks) through consistent periodic investments. Instead of making one lump-sum payment, the investment is divided into smaller, more manageable sums. While it doesn't assure a profit or guarantee against losses, it can help to reduce the effects of the market highs and lows. This is done by buying the same dollar amount in investments on a regular basis, regardless of the unit price.

One common example is a 401(k). Let's say you're investing in your 401(k) plan at work. Every two weeks, even before you get your paycheck, your 401(k) plan takes a portion from your check before you pay taxes or see any of that money, and uses those funds to purchase a certain dollar amount of a mutual fund or Exchange Traded Fund (ETF).

Every two weeks, the allocations are like clockwork. When the market is up, you buy shares at a higher price, but your previously purchased shares have also grown. When the market is down, your investment total may seem less impressive, but your money purchases more shares for a lower price than the prior ones. Those skinny shares will hopefully fatten when the market goes up again. Over time, it is a commonly used accumulation strategy designed to help grow your retirement account. Thus DCA (this consistent contribution) is viewed as a more effective investment strategy than if you would have stored up all those contributions and tried to time the market by putting it all in on one day and trying to ride the market roller coaster that way.

> The average American isn't saving much of their paycheck—most Americans don't have enough to cover a single $1,000 emergency. You can't retire on that. As a woman, I suggest shoot for closer to 14 percent of your paycheck going into your company's retirement plan (yet, ultimately, this does depend on your unique circumstances and time frame to retirement). You pay yourself first, not the IRS.
>
> That is the beauty of a company retirement plan (401(k), 403(b), TSP, SEP-IRA, etc.). You allocate money to your retirement savings BEFORE the IRS gets its hands on it (so you also pay less in current taxes). It is a great way to save automatically and efficiently. If you save 3, 4, or 6 percent from each paycheck, try to increase your contribution by 1-2 percent each year until you are at or above 14 percent. Most company plans have a feature that allows you to automatically increase your contribution by a certain percentage (say 1 percent) on a day of the year you determine (like the date when you receive a raise or bonus each year). Use it!

REVERSE DOLLAR COST AVERAGING (RDCA)

Well, sad to say, DCA works in reverse as well. Reverse dollar-cost averaging, or RDCA, is when you are making consistent withdrawals from your accounts or selling off shares. When the market is up, you are selling fewer shares, but when the market is down, you must sell off more shares to be able to meet your expenses (consider selling in March 2009, the lowest point in the market following the Great Recession), which also gives your account fewer assets to use to recover when the market bounces back.

So, is there another option when we want guaranteed income that doesn't exhibit RDCA?

Indeed, there is!

THE CERTAIN WAY

Then there is the second option. You can add a level of certainty into your retirement income plan by implementing some form of guaranteed income by designating an amount of your retirement assets toward income creation. Various tools are specifically designed to generate income for retirees, similar to how a pension works.

Most everyone has heard about annuities, but do we know what they really are, and how valuable a tool they can be? Annuities are a sort of pension for someone without a pension, and they can be used as a very intelligent income planning investment tool.

When you work for a company that offers a pension, you usually have an option to take it in a lump sum or to receive it as an annuity (the term annuity means "fixed annual sum for the remainder of the annuitant's life"). Most people don't question the credibility of the annuity being offered by Boeing or the City of Seattle pension provider. But if you're like most of us and don't have a pension, then you should consider evaluating an alternative income option that also offers a guaranteed income for life: *an annuity.*

Even though pensions pay guaranteed annual income using corporate annuities, we often see individuals conditioned to believe that all annuities are bad. Not so. You need to know the differences between them, and which ones might best fit your needs.

VARIABLE ANNUITIES

Often when I speak about purchasing a guaranteed income annuity, a woman's face distorts, her body language shifts, and she says, "Yuck, I don't like annuities. I hear annuities are bad." It could be because some annuities are not suitable for retirees on a fixed income. Annuities have evolved over the years, so what you may know about them from decades ago is likely outdated (like how my nutritionist had to recondition me as an endurance athlete to understand that carbs are not the enemy—thanks 1980s—but they are also not all created equal). Let's cover the different types of annuities offered today.

Variable annuities (VA) are sold through brokerage channels with the positive features of lifetime income and the upside potential offered by the stock market (we all want that!). But what you need to understand is that they involve market risk and market-related fees. Variable annuities involve market participation by investing in underlying mutual funds. Seems glamorous—upside potential capable of gaining a lot in a raging bull market (super sexy)—but they can deliver a significant hangover if the market goes through a major correction (not at all fun, that's why I gave up drinking years ago). The amount you gave to the insurance company (your principal amount) could lose value if the stock market tanks.

Additionally, there are three common types of variable annuity fees to be aware of:

1. Insurance fees, also known as mortality expense (M&E) fees, and administrative fees.

2. Investment management fees, similar to management fees on mutual funds.

3. Rider fees, for optional guarantees that there may be an increase in payments each year by a pre-set percentage to help keep up with inflation.

Additionally, if you withdraw more than the amount allowed each year, typically somewhere between 5–10 percent, you may incur a surrender charge.

Many of the clients we worked with were paying 3–4 percent in fees to own their variable annuities. That's a significant cost before you receive any actual benefit from the annuity. Being on a fixed income in retirement (remember, you don't have a paycheck any longer), you need to be mindful of the fees you are paying out of your retirement assets (more on this in Chapter Eight). With variable annuities' high fees and high market risk, variable annuities are not something I recommend for many pre- or post-retirees—retirement is a time to lower both fees and market risk.

IMMEDIATE ANNUITIES

Immediate annuities are another type of annuity. Immediate annuities provide the positive attribute of guaranteed income (which, again, we love) that begins immediately, and they don't carry stock market risk. But you give an amount of money to an insurance company, and they (not you) keep control over that money.

Control and options in retirement are paramount.

Often, immediate annuities have a certain amount of time that they guarantee payments, like five years, and if you die before the end of that time period, the insurance company sends your remaining payments to your named beneficiaries. But if you have an immediate annuity and you die in year six, in this example, the remaining principal balance will stay with the insurance company and not pay out to your beneficiaries. I don't like being out of control, and neither do you.

So, what are other possible positive options for retirement?

FIXED ANNUITIES

Fixed annuities are fixed (pre-determined) insurance products. They don't have downside market risk. Like all annuities, an insurance company (not a bank) issues the contract and for a set time period, say three to five years (that is the interest rate guarantee period). They have a declared interest rate that is generally 1 percent or so higher than what you could get at a bank for a Certificate of Deposit (CD), but usually in line with current interest rates for the country.

It often can be a great benefit for my clients in their late eighties, or into their nineties, for example. But the declared interest rate usually is not much higher than the inflation rate. So it doesn't get me too excited to put a big portion of money there if we need to use it for current or future income and to outpace inflation.

FIXED INDEX ANNUITIES

Maybe you are one of the millions who aren't fortunate enough to have a robust pension (like me), but you're looking for a financial vehicle that offers a similar stream of guaranteed income. I believe this income gap may be filled by fixed and guaranteed products (i.e., accounts that don't fluctuate with the market), which also allow you to control your principal. One such option that might be suggested, when it is prudent to do so, is a *fixed index annuity*, often with an optional guaranteed lifetime withdrawal benefit (GLWB) rider.

Fixed index annuities combine some of the upside potential for interest growth without being exposed to the downside risk of the market. They have the opportunity for steady, consistent income without losing control over your principal balance.

With a fixed index annuity, the costs of the product are built in, so you don't see added annual management fees or charges. The only fees you'll see deducted from your annuity value are for optional riders that you may select, such as the GLWB rider. These riders offer various features and guarantees, such as a potential increase in payments each year, or additional coverage for long-term care or other healthcare expenses.

SOUNDS GREAT, BUT WHAT'S THE CATCH?

Well, variable annuities and fixed index annuities are like any other financial product. There are terms, conditions, and limitations, and you need to decide if you can accept them, including a "surrender charge," which is a special fee that the insurance company might charge if you try to leave the contract early.

If you withdraw more than the amount allowed each year, typically somewhere between 5-10 percent, you may incur a surrender charge. There is a determined holding period (a period you are required to keep that contract with the insurance company) ranging from five to ten years for most annuities. If you pull out more money than the allotted amount, you may be charged a surrender penalty, in addition to ordinary income taxes payable. However, this fee is usually avoidable with proper planning.

This charge does not apply at death. Fixed index annuities become fully liquid at your death, so your heirs can usually receive the full remaining death benefit with no surrender penalties. We refer to them as having *limited liquidity,* since they have a holding period of up to ten years. That's one reason I would caution clients about not overdoing it; you want a good balance in your overall portfolio, and not too much of anything—even a good thing.

If you add a proper dosage of one of these steady products into a well-diversified plan, it can do the job to generate income for you during retirement, similar to how a pension would have if you had been lucky enough to have one.

NO PERFECT TOOL

No matter what type of financial investment tool you use, you can only have two out of these three attributes: *growth potential, liquidity, and protection*. Nothing in the investment world offers all three at once.

Growth Potential and Liquidity: This will typically be your investment or brokerage account. You get the market's upside potential with the ability to cash it in at any time and get most or all your money in a few days. But the downside is there isn't any safety component to it; there is no floor. If we hit another 2008-esque event, you could find yourself set back a couple of years or more and be emotionally (and financially) exhausted.

Liquidity and Protection: This will likely be your bank and money market money. It is readily available and FDIC-insured. This is a vital part of a healthy retirement plan. Confident spending typically comes from our accessible cash on hand. Most clients need a reasonable amount of liquid cash available at any given time, and the amount will vary by the client's situation. This is usually the account you draw out of for travel, gifting, fixing the water heater, or anything you desire to do now. The downside is you may receive close to "point nothing" in interest to have it just sitting there. Not much growth.

Protection and Growth Potential: This is where fixed index annuities fall. You get the opportunity to earn interest tied to an external market index but, because it's guaranteed by the issuing insurance company, and your annuity value won't decrease due to a market decline. Up or flat, but not down (unless it has a fee for an income rider, but that is not due to market loss). This can be a great component for a pre-

or post-retiree, but one of the downsides is they lack the liquidity piece. You can cash it out at any time, but just like with a CD, you will pay the penalty for doing so in the early years of the contract. As I mentioned before, they have limited liquidity since there is a determined surrender charge or "holding" period of five, seven, or ten years for most.

TAKES A VILLAGE

When it comes to a significant other, one person can't humanly meet every single need for you, and, in the same way, no one single investment tool can do all the work in your financial plan. But with great friends, family, church, clubs, medical professionals, mentors, pastors, etc., you can create a life that has all the important areas covered. You can live with great joy, peace, and health. A well-designed financial plan can help you do the same. Combining the right tools for you and your goals will give you the ultimate results.

BUILD YOUR LIFE ON A SOLID FOUNDATION

After successfully imploding my life at twenty-four, I had a lot of time ahead of me to rebuild and re-craft. If you (or someone else) sink your ship at sixty-five, you really don't have the luxury of a do-over. You don't want to get this *retirement thing* wrong. You need to take solid, well-founded advice from someone who specializes in planning for people fifty and above, because the investment rules you ran by in your twenties, thirties, and early forties don't necessarily apply when you're in your fifties, sixties, and beyond.

> *"You can be young without money, but you can't be old without it."*
> – TENNESSEE WILLIAMS

If you are interviewing a retirement planner or financial advisor and all they talk about is return on investments, stocks, bonds, and variable annuities, then run! Fast! If the conversation only centers around annuities and insurance, you are also limiting your success. Keep looking.

Be reminded of the three foundational pillars of retirement that I spoke about earlier:

1. *Preservation of assets:* Guarding the money you worked so hard to accumulate and being sure it will be there for your whole life (not just for most of your life).

2. *Income planning:* Using products and strategies that cover income gaps and planning to give you predictable paychecks to help you pay bills and have *play-checks* to enjoy the opportunities life affords you.

3. *Growth:* Once the areas of your needs and essentials (the concrete and the intangible) are covered, use strategies aimed at growth to address longevity, inflation, future healthcare, and legacy needs.

RULE #1: DON'T LOSE MONEY. RULE #2: DON'T FORGET RULE #1.

That is Warren Buffet's famous rules of investing. Buffet's wisdom becomes critical in retirement because losses are harder to recoup. Your lifespan shortens, and you have less capacity for risk (I address this more in Chapter Eight). It's not the time to bet the farm or to act in the same manner you did when you were trying to accumulate your retirement savings in your earlier years.

It bears repeating. We need to make sure growth remains in its proper place.

WHAT IS A GOOD ASSET MIX?

Ideally, you'll have some portion of your portfolio that will be stable, another portion that has modest upside opportunity with good cash flow and liquidity, and another portion poised for growth that will help you combat inflation.

Finding the right balance across asset classes is key. From that point, you can begin selecting the individual tools within each asset category, all the while keeping the theme of preservation in mind. In retirement, slow and steady returns win the race.

Certainly, any solid plan needs to be monitored and adjusted periodically, so I suggest revisiting your plan at least annually. Above all, trust your gut. If you still feel like you have too much money at risk, speak to your advisor until your portfolio is re-balanced so you can live at peace without hyperventilating each time the stock market ticker comes on the TV.

I'll end with this: I once had the opportunity to dive with sting rays and black-tipped reef sharks in the tropics. It was pouring rain, and the water was choppy. The guides assured us that diving in this kind of weather was perfectly safe, although the menacing storm told a different story. I was hesitant and a bit nervous, but the moment I was just a couple feet below the surface, I forgot about the raging storm completely. I didn't even notice it. I imagine farther out in the ocean, even the stronger squalls with tossing and roiling waves don't matter much to the marine life farther down below.

If your investments are appropriately placed, even with a serious market event, you can still weather the storm with relative ease and calm and enjoy some fun sights along the way. Effective planning is your personal insurance policy to ensure that everything is going to be okay. Work with a trustworthy financial advisor who can help do the heavy lifting and don't let your fears get in the way. There are wise options to help plan for the unique and wonderful life that you deserve!

> *You can't get where you are going without leaving where you've been.*

MOST IMPORTANT TAKEAWAYS

1. Income overlaid with expenses is the crux of planning. What you have saved for retirement is second to that. Stop comparing your unique situation to others and get the facts about your personal circumstances.

2. Mind the Gap—make sure you have a written income plan and can adequately answer where your income is coming from in retirement.

3. Inheritance is a bonus, so don't plan with it in mind. A fun part-time job may be exactly what you need to pad your retirement picture perfectly.

4. Get all the facts about the Social Security benefits due to you (especially if married or divorced after a ten-plus year marriage); the same goes for your pension.

5. Shoot to save 14 percent (or more) in your company retirement plan or SEP-IRA and have an annual increase automated if that feature is available.

6. Not all annuities are the same. Understand the different types available and how they work to decide if one might be right for you.

7. Growth, protection, liquidity—you can only have two of three in any one type of financial tool.

8. As you enter your mid-fifties, you need to begin shifting your mindset from growth, saving, and accumulation to preservation, income, then growth. Slow and steady.

NEXT STEPS

1. Find out how much money you will need once you stop working and have your financial advisor commit this income plan to paper. For married couples, be sure this plan works (again, on paper) even when you account for the death of your spouse or partner at any age. I know it sounds hard, but please have that conversation with your financial advisor or planner about the impact of how a premature death of you or your spouse would affect your long-term financial security. Don't shy away from this.

2. Ask your planner to show you how to optimize your Social Security and/or pension within the context of your plan, not in a micro-climate.

3. Right now, pull up your company retirement plan website to check your account, and consider increasing annual contributions by 1 percent. See if there is a feature that will do this automatically for you annually. Use it because every little bit counts (and it gets us out of the way of *getting 'round to it*).

4. If you are facing an income gap, ask your planner if an annuity could fill in the gap.

CHAPTER 8

MARKET RISK & FEES

Trials do not define, they refine.

SHE CUT HOW MUCH OFF YOUR HAIR?

I was twenty-two-years old before I let anyone other than my mom cut my hair. I have always had long hair, and I recall girls coming to school in junior high with short haircuts and shouting, "I went to the salon and she cut eight inches off my hair!" I had such a fear that I would go into a salon and some lady would chop my hair off (and get paid for it!) that I never went. When I was finally out of college and married, it seemed a bit weird to still let Mom cut my hair. I also realized I simply needed to communicate with my stylist about my preferences.

It sounds cliché, but communication is key.

If I go into the salon and say, "I want a change. Something a bit edgy," the stylist's idea of "change" and "edgy" could be totally different than mine. I don't want to leave with a turquoise mohawk.

Understanding risk is the same way. An individual may say, "I am a pretty moderate investor," but with a formal risk analysis, many of them test more conservative than they thought. If I took what she said, and applied my educated opinion of risk, I might just "chop off her hair," leaving her angry and disappointed at the next market correction.

That choice could alter your entire retirement.

"How do you feel about risk, from one to ten?"

"Hmm..." you may answer, "Three."

But what does that really mean? Conservative? Is that 30 percent? Are you okay with 30 percent of your retirement money at risk? Do you think a 30 percent drop in your savings is fine? Applying a simple percentage in the assessment of risk is too vague. Nonetheless, planners across the country ask that question and then act on those assumptions, often putting you in a position that is too risky or (much rarer, but still detrimental) too conservative. You need to have a much clearer determination of risk.

How much of your retirement assets (in dollars and cents) are you willing to put on the *craps table* that is the stock market? How much are you potentially willing to lose over the next six months? Answer that question, and you'll start to have some clear direction toward developing a retirement plan that's right for you.

> *"Decide whether or not the goal is worth the risks involved.*
> *If it is, stop worrying."* – AMELIA EARHART

CERTIFICATES OF DEPOSIT TO ELON MUSK

There are exceptional and simple tools that help to identify your risk. For years our firm used a tremendous program called Riskalyze (there are many risk analysis software products out there that can paint a similar picture, but I will use Riskalyze for the sake of this discussion). Riskalyze has risk numbers ranging from 1, which is *guaranteed*, to 99, most *aggressive* (complete lack of any guarantee). Guaranteed investments would entail cash, CDs, fixed annuities, and fixed index annuities. None have any risk of market loss (CDs and bank accounts are insured by the banks and the Federal Deposit Insurance Corporation (FDIC), and annuities are guaranteed by Annuity and Insurance Guaranty Association of the state you purchased the annuity in). Then you move up the risk ladder (the number gets larger) through bonds, REITs, variable annuities, and stocks to hang out with your buddy, Elon Musk, and his company, Tesla, at a risk number of 99.

Riskalyze works by dissecting your portfolio and individually assessing the fees and risk you take with each annuity, REIT, CD, stock, ETF, bond, mutual fund, etc. Based on the way these products all work together, the software assigns your household risk score an overall risk score from 1 to 99.

Your household risk score tells you what portion of your assets could potentially drop or go up in the next six months, and by how much. Often, those calculations will make a woman begin to sweat or feel sick to her stomach, as if it is actually happening. It's a visceral reaction and, candidly, it should be. This is all the money you must sustain your lifestyle for the rest of your life. Any pain you feel should inspire you to act.

Your household risk score is critical in helping you avoid those micro-climate plans we discussed. An advisor shouldn't make suggestions regarding your IRA or brokerage account that might duplicate investments you already have in a 401(k) at work. It could be shortsighted to pursue a hefty annuity contract if you'll be drawing a sizable pension from your work or your spouse's. You need to be sure that you're considering all your holdings, even if the advisor you're working with can't or doesn't personally manage all of them.

HOW MUCH ARE YOU REALLY WILLING TO LOSE?

So now that you have determined your *household risk score,* you need to understand the second part: your risk tolerance score. The software will now look at your total retirement asset value (not your net worth or home value, but the value of all your accounts—banking, brokerage, investment, annuity, etc.) and use that to determine your risk tolerance score. So, the amount of money you have for retirement, a dollar figure, is going to help the program identify questions specific to you to drill down as to the amount of money you are willing to *potentially* lose in the next six months if a major market correction occurred. Or, let me put it this way: you open your brokerage statement, and you see that you have lost X amount of money in the last six months. It's not just in terms of percentages; it in terms of dollars and cents, a subtle shift that can radically change the way people think and talk about their risk tolerance.

RISK TOLERANCE VERSUS RISK CAPACITY

There's a big difference between risk tolerance and risk capacity. Emotionally you might be able to tolerate risk and say, "Yeah, I can handle losing 25 percent." But, as a financial advisor, I might say, "Your retirement doesn't have the capacity for that. You do that and you could face the risk of running out of money before your time." You don't want that to happen. You must get your risk tolerance and risk capacity in line based on other factors in your life.

Remember Lily from Chapter Five? Her specific story speaks to many of the components of risk. She was the gal who suddenly lost her husband at fifty-nine. Lily hadn't worked for many years due to raising children and caring for her ailing mother. She was part of the *sandwich generation,* as a woman who was concurrently caring for children and ailing parent.

When we finally dug into the specifics of Lily's financial situation, I discovered that she had $800,000 in retirement savings—that was great! 100 percent of that money was from her husband's company plan and their investment brokerage account. There was no pension, no life insurance proceeds, and the smaller of the two Social Security benefits stopped coming upon her husband's death. Not having a pension is common these days, and the loss of a spouse's Social Security is inevitable. But you can always have some form of life insurance. We will talk about that in Chapter Eleven, but adequate insurance is one tool that can make a serious difference in keeping widows out of poverty.

Lily's $800,000 was everything to her and would need to last for possibly another forty years. Remember, she was fifty-nine. You may recall, her two highest priorities were never needing to return to work and never burdening her kids with her care. The thought of putting her kids through that hell made her skin crawl.

FINANCIAL SECURITY MEANT EVERYTHING TO HER. EVERYTHING.

As we talked, I discovered her and her James's assets had peaked at approximately $800,000 in 1999, followed by three years of "dot-bomb" losses (2000, 2001, 2002) that dropped their total by hundreds of thousands. Their accounts finally climbed back to the $800,000 watermark when I met her in June 2008. When I began a deep dive into what Lily had as investments, I realized she had a lot of concentrated stock in many beloved Northwest companies. I love supporting Northwest companies, but as my husband says, "too much of a good thing can make you sick or broke!" This led us into a serious conversation about market risk.

Since the "dot-bomb" correction, Lily wasn't just widowed, but she was now six years older. Half a decade can make a big difference in the time-horizon of a plan, and she realized that her accounts were much too volatile for her risk tolerance (emotional capacity to handle risk) and risk capacity (monetary capacity to handle risk).

So, let's see how this exercise looked for Lily...

"Looking California, Feeling Minnesota" is a line that the late vocalist Chris Cornell of the band Soundgarden (I grew up in Seattle during the nineties grunge era) wrote as he felt a bit frumpy but caught a glance of himself in the mirror wearing surfing board shorts and a T-shirt. That echoes this sense of living aggressively but feeling conservative. I think that when comparing those two states, that line could very much have applied to Lily's situation regarding risk; "looking aggressive, feeling conservative" seemed to be an apt description. Lily's household risk score was 74, but her risk tolerance score was 31, a massive discrepancy!

"Okay, Lily, we need to do some re-balancing of your current holdings to get your entire investment household in line with your risk tolerance score of 31. It could be a major blow to your retirement portfolio if you went through a significant market gyration when you are living a 74 (looking aggressive) but desiring a 31 (feeling conservative)."

GETTING BACK IN ALIGNMENT

Looking aggressive but feeling conservative. Grounds for emotional and possibly financial destruction. She agreed that a significant change was in order. So, I began to show her ways we could correct her incongruity through re-balancing of her portfolio.

So how may this apply to you? You have worked with blinders on, contributing to your company plan, and the Great Recession has been in the rear-view mirror for quite some time. If you haven't had a re-balancing discussion, I implore you to discuss with your advisor your current risk posture and how it does (or doesn't) fit with the way you are invested. I have sat with hundreds of women who have just left their assets alone for years or even more than a decade. The equity positions (growth stocks) did very well, whereas bonds (less risky income producers) performed poorly during a period of low interest rates, and this caused an out-of-balance portfolio that began to shift out of the investment posture they were comfortable with a few years earlier.

Make sure you are revisiting your risk posture every couple of years; this helps to make sure your assets are still in line with what you can emotionally tolerate.

Remember our three foundational pillars of retirement planning: preservation of assets, income planning, and then growth. Those pillars need to stay in the proper order when you are in or nearing retirement, and they can only do that when you have a clear plan based on sound research and experience—not just what worked in the past. Financial catastrophes can be prepared for. It is possible to weather even another recession if preservation is always first and foremost in the plan.

Back to Lily.

Once we had identified her risk tolerance score, we began to evaluate the *what-ifs* of longevity, nursing home care, or a major market correction. We hope to virtually eliminate any possibility of a running out of money before age 100, or at least push it out as far as we can with good planning, proper investments, and behavioral coaching. For her, the changes we suggested were intended to potentially remove her risk of ever running out of money.

Lily was ready to handle it.

We began crafting a personalized retirement plan for her. She marveled at the simplicity of the outline and how easy it was for her to understand, and I could see her confidence growing. We started the initial process of bringing her assets over to our custodian and under our care, and then spent the rest of the visit talking about scripture verses and quotes she was considering to place on a memorial bench for her husband at a park near their home.

She left our office with hugs. Victory!

Until...

Two days later, she called with apologies.

"You know, Arwen, thank you so much for the effort. I really appreciate all your help, but I'm going to cancel the new plan. I talked to my son, and he said that it sounded too conservative. He isn't familiar with some of the investment tools you talk about, and he wanted me to talk to our previous advisor, first."

Sheepishly, she felt obligated to take her son's advice. He wanted her to get into contact with the gentleman that her husband had set things up with more than fifteen years before. To appease her son, she gave the advisor a call, and tried her best to explain the updated retirement plan I had proposed for her. Imagine Lily, being completely detached from her finances for all those years, trying to explain her new financial direction (and we'd had only three visits together) to a seasoned investment professional. It would be like reading the glove-box manual to a new car and trying to drive it on a California freeway without even having a driver's license. Impossible.

Once he had her on the phone, he was not about to lose the $800,000 of hers that he was currently charging advisory fees on. He threw every possible punch to try and retain Lily as a client, and told her that annuities were bad and our plan was not good for her. He went as far as to say that her original plan was the one that her husband had in mind. "Your husband trusted me all those years," he said, "I hope you would, too." That would make any widow feel guilty, supposedly betraying the wishes of her beloved husband. In the end, Lily was afraid to upset her son or the advisor, and she backed out on the chance to finish her new financial and life plan with us.

Yet, here is the fact: 73 percent of women leave their financial advisors following the death of their spouse within the first year, because they didn't have good communication or a comfortable relationship[28]. Lily was no different; she didn't feel connected to the former planner and that is why she wanted to work with us.

---

28 Billows, Kristen. "Don't Give Female Clients Reason To Leave." Financial Advisor, October 4, 2022. https://www.fa-mag.com/news/don-t-give-female-clients-reason-to-leave-69978.html

But she stayed with the former advisor and the plan that we had clearly identified as too risky for her. In my opinion, it was a mistake to question herself and betray her intuition.

That was June of 2008. Within a few short months, the stock market experienced the worst decline in her living history. Her $800,000 in retirement assets and financial security sank by nearly half ($350,000)!

LEARNING FROM HER MISTAKES

The key takeaways from Lily's story are that she was not listened to, nor was she properly educated or informed from the start. Lily was talked down to and manipulated. She had been working with a salesman—not a trusted advisor. She was being told what to do, not *co-creating* a plan with her retirement planner. And she made the classic error of subjugating herself and letting others make her decisions for her.

When you have a clear financial life plan based on your values, sound research, and wise experience (not just what feels convenient or what worked in the past), you can avoid catastrophes like this.

I have Lily on my mind, to this day—did she have to go back to work? Was she forced to sell her home and move in with her son? What compromises has she had to make? Is she okay? Sadly, Lily would never get to take her grandchildren on the Disney cruise they all dreamed about. She likely had to put all her personal goals aside to survive and take care of the basics. That hurts.

Her downturn was preventable, and that's a painful truth.

I urge you, as a woman, to take part in your financial future and get what you need. Don't settle, don't let yourself feel pressured, and please don't let anyone make your decisions for you.

TRUST YOUR GUT

Women's intuition is a powerful higher level of consciousness. It is an invaluable blend of emotional, intellectual, psychic, and spiritual impressions. It may not give you a specific and direct message, but it's there to wake you up and ask you to pay attention. Intuition prompts us towards survival. It's been called a sixth sense that warns us against danger, as well as our natural "guardian angel." Now, you may not completely comprehend all the ins and outs of personal finance, but you do have a direct connection with your intuition. If something doesn't feel right, listen to that feeling, slow things down, and ask more questions. You did it to take care of your kids when things just seemed *off*—please apply it to your financial life, too.

Many women get derailed when listening to the opinions and orders of others, and ignore their gut intuition because it doesn't wear a business suit and tie. If you have an advisor, family member, or friend who is pressuring you to do something that doesn't feel right, remember that this is *your money* and *your future.* Make sure you feel peace and ease with the advisor you are in dialogue with. Remember that a financial advisor is absolutely key, but that he or she is not there to make decisions for you. Don't betray yourself and your own natural system when it speaks.

"A woman knows by intuition, or instinct, what is best for herself."
– MARILYN MONROE

IT'S TIME IN THE MARKET, NOT TIMING THE MARKET

"Arwen, call us first thing tomorrow—we want to liquidate everything to cash!"

The time stamp on that voicemail was 11:43 PM on Donald Trump's election night. I called those clients back the next day and did my best to deter them from making such a rash, emotionally-based decision, but they wouldn't budge. I called the trading desk and instructed them to liquidate the $320,000 they had invested in the stock market to cash.

That began one of the best first one hundred days in the market of a presidential term.

The problem with timing the market is you must be right *twice*. You need to be right when planning to get out, and you need to be right when getting back in. The problem is, no one ever knows when the market is going to go up or down. They can speculate, but the words *speculate* and *retirement* do not belong in the same sentence.

You're smart, and you know that. Trust yourself.

Retirement planning isn't about timing short bursts in and out of the market. You need a long-term strategy that allocates some money to risk and growth opportunity, and that has the time to recover when the market gyrates or corrects. Markets generally recover, at least to a certain extent. But the challenge is that we don't know how long that may take, and the correction may come at the worst time for you: at the beginning of your retirement journey.

When reviewing your financial plan (using a long-term perspective) there is an expectation and an understanding that the market will go through some kind of correction. Having those *what-if* conversations with your advisor will help prepare you for how to deal with them emotionally and tactically. Communicating with your advisor can prevent and heal some of that unease. You need to know why you have the plan, what to do, and how to handle it if the market goes awry—and this is the motivation behind doing a plan overview on a yearly basis. At the very least, it's a chance to proactively talk to your advisor and revisit reality again and again.

An advisor can run simulations with their program and help see how things would look *if, when,* and *what*—throwing arrows at it. You can take it out to the extreme, and see how the plan performs.

The couple who called on election night missed some of the best growth during those early Trump years because they made an emotional decision—not one based on healthy long-term planning.

Do not work with anyone who tells you they know how to time the market. The moment for rational, long-term planning begins now, not "when the market comes back."

You can't afford to play games with your life savings.

MORE OPTIONS IN AN IRA—IN-SERVICE DISTRIBUTION

Multiple times through the last ten years, I directed my mom to withdraw money out of her 401(k) at Costco and deposited those funds into her actively managed IRA. That action is called an *in-service distribution*. It's where you're still employed with your company and actively contributing to your company's retirement plan, but you can withdraw the money saved in your company plan, roll it into an IRA (not a bank account, so you don't cause a taxable event), and then you have additional investment options available to you, not just the limited few options in your company's plan. You typically *shouldn't* do an in-service distribution before turning fifty-nine-and-one-half, however, or you will receive a 10 percent penalty from the IRS (uh, no thank you).

My mom wanted these rollovers to lessen her concentrated investment in Costco stock, which was very aggressive (as of today, a risk number of 72). She wanted to start protecting those assets, to make sure they would be there for her after working extremely hard for fifty-two years. Many women I speak with are, like my mom, conservative investors. They cite financial security as their primary value. If that is you, it is often wise to turn to tools with some growth potential and little to no downside risk.

LESS RISK THE OLDER WE GET

Words I never hear as women begin to move towards retirement: "I want things to be riskier and more complicated." Oh, please. The older you get, the more risk-averse you become, and the greater your desire for simplicity and organization. Risk-reduction and management are the most common areas an advisor should focus on with new clients. It is not at all uncommon for a potential client, newly retired or just about ready to retire, and have 75 to 95 percent of their assets invested in the stock market. Historically, the market delivers the best growth potential, pound for pound, and is where most of us grow, accumulate, and save money for retirement. But nearing retirement, the percentages need to trend lower.

For example: one way to reduce risk it to take current investments and replace them with lower-risk investments. The management happens in two parts—the advisor looks over the accounts and sees where things can be allocated more safely as the client ages. The other part is more *active* management, which means you are invested in an account that has a management fee so as to have someone actively manage and "turn the dials" to keep that account within the risk posture you are comfortable with.

This would look like an investment in a large-cap growth fund. That outside individual will change out large-cap investments if one is under-performing with another large-cap investment. It would never be changed with a mid- or small-cap, or bonds (which are conservative, the opposite of growth), because that would change the overall design of it being a large-cap growth fund. Active management will, however, increase/decrease certain positions, while always being cognizant that the overall risk posture remains growth (not moderate or conservative). He or she will never change the overall risk posture (i.e., conservative, moderate or growth). Having the oversight of a financial advisor will help you understand these changes over time. Active management keeps the investment within your tolerance range while you focus on those things that truly matter.

RULE OF 100

Here is a very simple rule of thumb to determine if you need to think about shifting the proportion of assets you have at risk:

The *Rule of 100* is a general principle that states: *if you subtract your age from 100, the result is the percentage of your assets reasonable to invest at risk.* So, if you are sixty years old, you subtract your age from 100, and what you have remaining, 40, is the responsible percentage to keep at risk. If you are married, you average your ages and then do the same thing. If you have north of 70 percent of your retirement assets at risk, you should think strongly about moving a portion of your assets from a place of high risk to low risk or no risk.

As I said, it's just a general principle—factors such as the amount of assets you have, your legacy goals, your healthcare plans, your planned retirement date, and others will affect the picture.

When I was personally seeing clients, our team would perform a much more thorough analysis of risk tolerance and capacity, but at least this very simple "rule" can give you a little direction as you get closer to retirement. If you work with an advisor whose allocation recommendations are far off of the quick marginal calculation of the *Rule of 100,* ask why and be sure they have a very satisfactory answer that you agree with.

LOTS OF EGGS, LOTS OF BASKETS

Now that you have a good indication of how much money to retain in a position of accelerated growth potential and risk, we want to make sure those assets are more broadly diversified. When you are looking at ways to keep growth potential in your retirement plan, you want broad diversification, which means a lot of eggs in a lot of baskets.

To be clear, an asset is a resource that you own or control that has economic value. It is anything that can be used or liquidated to produce a future value. Some examples of assets include cars, cash, real estate, a checking account, jewelry, investments, artwork, bonds, pensions, marketable securities, gold, and furniture, to name a few. The investment vehicles within your portfolio should include a mix of assets (the different kinds of investments you make) with a range of risk levels to make sure you are never too vulnerable in any one area.

Mutual funds, as well as ETFs (an exchange-traded fund) can provide very highly diversified options and can cover a great deal of financial landscape, so that if one area is burning to the ground, another area might just be rising from the ashes. That's broad diversification. But it doesn't have to be overly complicated; many accounts with broad diversification might have only fifteen to twenty mutual funds or ETF holdings (line items on your statement) that represent hundreds of investments. Women don't want to get sixty-two-page statements; they want them to be simplified, yet balanced, and diversification is the best way to lessen your potential harm from a market correction.

How much you are paying your advisor?

"How much do you pay your financial advisor to manage this account?" That's a common question I would ask prospective clients. Many women can answer that question. They'll say something like 1 percent or 1.5 percent. Other times, they aren't entirely sure.

I had this gal come in who had $1.5 million managed by a professional, so I asked, "Well, how much do you pay the advisor to manage that?"

She hesitated, then said, "Well, I think about $300 a month."

I looked at her, bewildered, and responded, "I am sorry, my dear, but I don't think that any advisor would manage that amount of money for only $300 a month. Can I see a statement?"

My client got online and pulled off the statement. I looked through it and I said, "Well, I've got to tell you, we're about halfway through the year, and you've already paid about $9,000 in fees."

She was paying about six times more than she thought.

And those were just the fees that were visible on her statement...

FEES YOU CAN'T SEE

The truth is advisory fees are not bad if you're receiving value for them, but often it's the internal fees that individuals have zero clue about. Internal fees (internal expense ratios) are the administrative costs associated with a mutual fund, REIT, or ETF. For example, if you own a mutual fund, which is a big basket of holdings (i.e., stocks, bonds, etc.), there's a team of people "inside" that fund making decisions on your behalf. A little less here, little more there, kick that stock out, bring in this bond. When that happens, there are administrative costs paid to the people that manage it.

Unless you love to jump on the internet and research every mutual fund or ETF you own, most women are completely in the dark as to the amount they pay for internal expenses. You won't ever see these fees on your statements; instead, you need to read a fund's complex and lengthy prospectus to find this information. Any advisor worth their salt should show you early on in your relationship how much you pay internally for your entire household (every holding), and that is before the advisor managing it gets their cut in advisory fees.

It was not uncommon to see prospective clients with holdings that cost, internally, north of 2 percent. Sometimes I'd seen funds with costs at almost 4 percent! Add a 4 percent expense ratio to a 1.5 percent advisory fee, and you need to gross 5.5 percent just to break even. This is expensive and, in most cases, completely unnecessary.

To be clear, unless you are a broker who can spend time privately negotiating trade deals for each stock with a company, the services that each layer of management provides on your behalf are completely necessary. You can't get something for nothing. But it's also true that you should get what you pay for. If one company charges you 3 percent, they better darn well be able to explain why they are so much better than the one down the street charging 1 percent. In my experience, most can't and don't.

Once you retire, I urge you to try to keep the internal fees below 0.6 percent. Since you are on a fixed income once you retire, anything that robs your growth and sends money somewhere other than your pocket is affecting your overall financial returns. Ultimately, your returns are your retirement.

Know your numbers. It matters. You matter.

> *Belief without effort is a total waste of time. You must back up your faith with action.*

MOST IMPORTANT TAKEAWAYS

1. 70 percent of women leave their financial advisors following the death of their spouse[29].

2. Risk tolerance is your emotional ability to handle risk, and risk capacity is how much your money can handle.

---

29 https://www.kiplinger.com/personal-finance/604133/for-widows-3-life-changing-financial-resolutions#:~:text=Up%20to%2070%25%20of%20widows,death%2C%20according%20to%20Vanguard%20research.

3. Trust your gut intuition, even if you don't understand why it is sounding. Ask your questions without fear of judgment. If you can't ask those questions without fear, find a new advisor.

4. It is time in the market, not timing the market. That strategy requires you to be right twice. Those aren't good odds in your favor.

5. Most companies allow an in-service distribution from your company plan at fifty-nine-and-one-half without penalty, and it can be a great idea with more investment choices available inside an IRA than you will have inside your company's plan.

6. The *Rule of 100* is a simple way to estimate the reasonable risk for your current age.

7. Commonly misunderstood fees include the expenses you can't see on your statement for the investments you own. Ask questions.

8. Broad diversification and simplicity are beautiful words in retirement.

NEXT STEPS

1. If you aren't sure of the relationship with your advisor and you are married, either reach out to have a meeting (maybe one-on-one) to make sure you build that communication, or have the tough conversation with your spouse about looking for an advisor that connects well with both of you. You deserve to feel heard.

2. At your next meeting (call and set one up, if necessary), have your advisor identify your true risk tolerance in dollars and cents as it relates to your retirement assets. If your advisor doesn't test for this, I suggest you look for someone who does.

3. Re-balance your portfolio immediately if it's no longer in line with your desired risk tolerance. Make sure you discuss your risk tolerance with your advisor and that they can show you how your current holdings are clearly in line with how you now feel about risk, not how you felt eighteen months ago. You may need to retest your tolerance.

4. If you are approaching or are fifty-nine-and-one-half, ask your advisor what they would recommend for you regarding an in-service distribution of your company plan.

5. Take some time to sit down and write out all the questions and worries you have on your mind. The economy, politics, gas prices, elections, family issues, Social Security questions—all of it. Send an email to your advisor that lists some of these and tell your advisor "These are some of the things I'd like to discuss in our next meeting, thank you." Release the pressure and utilize your advisor as needed—you don't have to wait until an emergency or the annual review to ask your questions. That's the foundation of a good advisor relationship—be proactive. The advisor won't get their feelings hurt.

6. Ask your advisor to remind you what their advisory/management fees are to manage your assets and to do a complete fee analysis for your entire household of investments. If they can't, find an advisor who can.

CHAPTER 9

TAXES & REQUIRED MINIMUM DISTRIBUTIONS

> *Before the battle with your hands comes the battle in your mind.*

25 PERCENT OFF: GREAT FOR A NORDSTROM SALE, NOT PENALTIES

"Didn't your advisor tell you to take your RMDs?" By the look on her face, you could see she had no idea what Randy was talking about. Years ago, we brought on a full-service tax practice that afforded us the ability to have a certified public accountant (CPA) to prepare individual and business returns for our clients and many folks in our community, while adding great value to our existing clients. This woman was discussing her 1040 tax return with Randy before she took it home, but (at the time) she was not a retirement planning client of ours.

Randy continued as he poured over the woman's tax return from the previous year. "I should have seen some income on this line right here for your IRA. Now that you're seventy-three, you should have taken your Required Minimum Distribution (RMD) from your IRAs last year." As Randy looked at the woman's year-end statements, he found that, according to the IRS's life expectancy table, she should have withdrawn $15,000 from her IRA for her RMD.

She hadn't needed the additional income for her living expenses, so she hadn't thought to make the withdrawal. Failure to do so had cost her a hefty penalty—one of the largest penalties in the tax code: 25 percent! Let me repeat, the IRS takes a 25 percent penalty of missed RMDs. For this woman, $3,750 of her missed RMD went straight to Uncle Sam!

You will spend a great deal of your life accumulating much of your wealth in *qualified plans*—401(k)s, 403(b)s, 401(a)s, TSPs, etc.—or Individual Retirement Accounts—IRAs, SIMPLE-IRAs, SEP-IRAs, etc. These are wonderful vehicles for saving money and accumulating wealth. You are taking a portion of your paycheck and paying yourself first (even before the sneaky IRS gets its hands in it). Then, the IRS will take its cut of what's left of your paycheck, and you get to take home what remains. Saving this way, you pay less in taxes along the journey because the IRS hasn't taken its cut of those retirement funds yet.

Operative word: *yet*.

You have delayed paying taxes on your qualified plans your whole life and now the IRS wants its portion of your money and will demand it at the rate it feels is appropriate; hence the term *required minimum distribution*. You could pay taxes when the money goes in (the seed). That's what happens when you contribute to a Roth IRA—you pay taxes upfront and, if you abide by the terms of the plan, never have to worry about the IRS coming for those monies again. However, with *qualified plans*, you choose to take the current tax break allowed with a pre-tax contribution while working. So, the IRS will want its cut of the harvest. From that point forward, the IRS collects an RMD and will expect that payment every year for the rest of your life at the rate it determines appropriate.

The original SECURE Act of 2019 significantly increased the RMD age from age seventy-and-one-half to seventy-two. The updated SECURE 2.0 brought additional updates so that RMDs begin at age seventy-three for qualifying individuals who turn seventy-two years of age on or after January 1, 2023. And in ten more years, 2033, the RMD age shifts from age seventy-three to seventy-five. My response to the government: geez, make up your minds! Again, having a financial professional partner with you on this issue is vital to getting it right the first time.

As for the example of my client at the beginning of this chapter, the previous advisor's oversight cost her $3,750. That would have paid for a three-week cruise for many of our more frugal clients. What a rip-off! This is one of the consequences of neglectful planning.

LET'S AVOID A 25 PERCENT MISTAKE

As planners who focus specifically on retirement, this RMD tax bomb looming in the distance must be a constant focus. Even if you are fifty-five, this should be a topic of discussion with the advisor you are working with. You can do considerable tax planning seven to twenty years away from that RMD time period, but once you hit it, there is little left but to take it and pay the tax (unless you want to give it all to charity). I understand that this is very much a first-world problem, but you don't want to find yourself in the same boat as many older clients who pay more in taxes at age seventy-five than they ever did while they were working. This is a one of the main reasons why you want strategic integrated planning—not tactics handled in a micro-climate.

Your advisor will be looking at the future while your CPA reports the past and a combination of those points of view will give you the best possible comprehensive plan. Find an advisor who either has a CPA on staff or who at least runs a tax simulation to give you an idea of what your situation will look like. Any retirement planner worth their weight in gold will have your tax situation in mind and will be prepared to show you how much you are going to be paying according to current rates used by the IRS.

Financial advisors work with people, not just money, and if you are with an advisor who has not spoken to you about your future tax bill and provided ideas and direction for how to reduce it, I would think long and hard about that relationship. Are they truly the best resource for you over the long term?

On occasion, a woman might struggle with the idea of changing advisors. We would often hear, "Well, I will have to go back to my (current) advisor and ask them why we haven't talked about this and what to do about my RMD." My question back to her at that moment was always, "I understand what you mean, but doesn't it concern you that *you* must initiate discussion on that topic with your advisor? Isn't that their job, as the expert, to bring to your attention what you need to do? It would make me wonder what other things they might be missing or failing to mention."

PROACTIVE NOT REACTIVE

After selling our company, Randy and I were looking for a top-notch CPA firm to help us as we had more significant tax planning than prior to the sale. We wanted to find someone who would help us brainstorm ideas on long-term tax saving strategies, who understood alternative investment options, and who would actively involve with legacy planning for our kids and grandkids. For over a year, we had been scouting for just the right person. The CPA we had before selling the firm said that what we wanted and needed was out of her wheelhouse, but she referred us to someone very smart with great experience.

We took her advice and started working with this individual, eager to get things rolling. Then, in late November—the end of the year—Randy sent him an email to ask if there was anything else we might do to reduce our tax bill. Time was running out, and we had just finished the sale of our practice. This was a major life (and taxable) event for us, and it had been an extremely busy year! We had a lot on our minds.

The CPA replied to us saying, "No, I think we're good. See you after the first of the year!"

We were dumbfounded. That's it? We wanted someone to come to the table with dynamic solutions for how to reduce our taxes, and how to accommodate our recent life changes. This individual had no ideas, and wasn't even eager to have a conversation. "See you next year" was not a comforting message. He was promptly fired, and we found the CPA we needed, but sadly the year had already concluded, and the lack of planning post-sale cost us huge in taxes.

We could not go back and make up the time or ask the IRS for a do-over. Don't let your time window for great planning pass you by—begin having those conversations in your fifties and sixties while the strategies are still available to you. Just like selling a company, you don't get second chances to do things over again when you retire. You need a proactive approach with a great coach who specializes in retirement who will arm you with everything you need to get this right the first time (and on time!).

HOW IS IT CALCULATED?

The IRS has a tax table based on life expectancy that dictates you withdraw a certain percentage of your qualified plan total. In plain language, that means each year as you age, the IRS will require you to withdraw a specified amount (starting with a factor of 26.5 percent when you're seventy-three and decreasing each year to 2.0 percent for anyone 120 or older) from the combined total of your IRAs or similar plans[30]. For example, if your IRA had a value of $100,000, and you were seventy-three, you would divide it by the factor provided by the IRS Uniform Life Expectancy Table (for this example 26.5 percent), and would arrive at a distribution amount of $3,773.58. This simply translates to 3.77 percent distribution from your IRA to satisfy your RMD. There are examples where you must use a separate table (i.e., if your spouse is ten years older/younger than you or if other circumstances may apply), so please check with your advisor so you aren't slapped with a 25 percent penalty for getting it wrong.

SATISFIED AND CONTENT OR OVERSTUFFED AND MISERABLE

On Mother's Day morning, you forced yourself to stay on the treadmill a bit longer, choked down a bland protein shake for breakfast, and, by design, felt starved by noon. Church is over and you are now on your way in your oversized light pink sweater and stretchy slacks (with your Spanx hiding beneath) to the town's best brunch buffet for a Mother's Day celebration. Your kids and grandkids are treating you, and the spread is amazing. Prime rib, giant prawns, waffles with bananas, eggs benedict, mini crème brûlées—and that's just a small sampling of the yummy delights. Mmm! You knew this brunch was coming, and you did all you could to prepare for the large, wonderful meal that lay ahead.

You were creating a hunger gap and calculating your day around it.

We can apply this example to your RMDs.

You are now sixty-three and have enjoyed many years working as a schoolteacher, but your pension doesn't turn on till sixty-five, and you have determined you'd like to delay your Social Security till

---

[30] IRS website, "Retirement Topics — Required Minimum Distributions (RMDs)." https://www.irs.gov/retirement-plans/plan-participant-employee/retirement-topics-required-minimum-distributions-rmds

seventy. Your RMD lies ahead, like your Mother's Day brunch, but at this moment in time, there is a gap—a wonderful, beneficial gap.

I love these gaps, and so should you.

An income gap such as this is an ideal time to consider evacuating (using) some of the money in your qualified accounts—IRA, 403(b), 401(k)s, and such—while you have little to no income coming in (for the sake of this discussion we will lump everything into the term IRA). This means you are in a lower tax bracket, currently, so if you pull the income you need to bridge the income gap between the time your pension and Social Security begin to flow, you will pay a *lower rate* in taxes to use your IRA monies AND you will have a smaller tax bomb ahead of you when RMDs begin. Taking out some of the money in your retirement accounts while in a lower tax bracket is just good planning.

Or you could delay your RMD planning and have it go a bit more like this:

You consume a glazed pumpkin scone and grande mocha (extra whipped cream) at Starbucks just before church. At that point, 763 calories are firmly planted in your stomach, yet you will still feel obligated to eat the massive mid-morning brunch. The script plays in your head, "I never get these kinds of foods, and the kids went to all this trouble to bring me. It's expensive. I better eat more." We have all made that mistake before.

We pile in more food than we want, and we're left overstuffed and miserable.

This is a very common occurrence for retirees who pay more in taxes at seventy-five than when they were working. They neglected proper planning while in their fifties and sixties. Now, they are collecting a pension, Social Security, and RMDs. When you are forced to pull out—and pay taxes on—income you *don't* need, it is frustrating. Maddening, in fact.

For some clients, this income gap also creates an ideal time to consider Roth conversions. Roth IRAs are a good opportunity for many because you pay taxes on the money going in (the seed), but the harvest accumulates and comes out tax-free! It can be tough to build up a Roth while you are in the life stage of saving and accumulating your wealth, which is why most of us have regular 401(k)s or IRAs. But, by gradually paying taxes on and converting some accounts to Roth IRAs, you'll have no RMDs, will not be taxed, and can even pass to beneficiaries tax-free.

So, if you were to convert Traditional IRA funds to a Roth IRA, you would pay taxes on all the funds you convert in a given year. Provided the Roth IRA has been open for at least five years, you can take any withdrawals after fifty-nine-and-one-half as tax-free money.

Paying less in taxes now and in the future is obviously the ideal situation, but you may need help knowing how to execute Roth IRA conversions and what path is right for you. Have your advisor or CPA run scenarios to determine how to maximize the income gap during your retirement. If you don't have a great relationship with your CPA, this is something your financial advisor can help you with (or at least give you proper guidelines for). Make sure you understand this concept when you are speaking with your financial advisor. Ask them what type of tax planning they do to help reduce your future tax bill. Your seventy-five-year-old self will thank you. Also, it's fun to stick your tongue out at the IRS and say, "Pbsst! Neener, neener, neener! I beat you!"

THAT WILL BE $90,000 IN TAX—BRING YOUR CHECKBOOK

Debbie and Ray had been clients of ours for more than ten years. They had been married for forty-five years and lived happily in their home for thirty-two years. When Ray began to struggle at finding his words and recalling elementary information, Debbie recognized that something wasn't right. A dementia diagnosis soon followed, and it was only a matter of eighteen months from there until she found herself afraid to leave her husband alone.

The terrible realization hit hard: *he needed to move into a long-term care facility.*

Debbie thus began the agonizing effort of moving her best friend into a facility near their home.

Their residence was more than she wanted to maintain alone, and it was a harsh reminder of her husband's absence. She decided it was time to sell the memories, both great and not-so-great. The pain of waking up without him near, along with the added pressure of living alone in a big house, was increasingly stressful. They had enjoyed so many great times together in that house, and she was very conflicted.

It was bittersweet, but she handled it.

The area that Debbie and Ray lived in was experiencing massive growth. In the 1980s, they had purchased their home for $300,000. When Debbie's real estate agent placed it on the market, it was snatched up nearly overnight for $1.4 million. WOW! Even factoring in $100,000 of improvements over the years (cost basis), they made about a million dollars from the sale. Of course, some of that was inflation value, right? Well, while the IRS cut them some slack by giving each of them an individual stepped up in basis of $250,000 (means the $300,000 + $100,000 (improvements) + $500,000 in stepped up basis (= $900,000), so they needed to pay taxes on the remaining $500,000). The result was that Debbie would need to cut the IRS a check for $90,000, as they had to pay capital gains tax on the remaining $500,000.

When she came in to consult Randy about the sale, she was in a state of shock as to where she should pull the $90,000 fund to pay the tab. Randy suggested that prior to liquidating some assets to pay the bill, she consult the CPA we had on staff to see if there was anything that could be done to reduce that tax liability, even by a thousand or two.

The CPA asked for her tax returns from the past five years and discovered a *gift* from the past. Many years ago, Ray had sold some stocks at a loss, creating a large capital loss that became a *future gift* to his wife, though at the time I'm sure Ray had been very disappointed.

The day that Debbie arrived at the office to finalize her planning and find out the conclusion of the CPA's findings, she had her checkbook and was reluctantly ready to write a $90,000 check to the IRS. The CPA, however, had some good news. Thanks to the capital loss from several years before, she would only have to pay $40,000.

Fifty thousand dollars saved!

She was shocked, because that remaining $50,000 meant she could pay for five months of her husband's long-term care, which was out of pocket. She was deeply grateful for the gift and for the professional wisdom that supported her. In difficult times like these, we want to be able to focus on caring for our loved ones, not trying to combat tax implications.

The net effect of tax efficiency is just unreal.

LESS TO IRS MEANS MORE FOR YOU

When you are on a fixed income in retirement (no longer getting a paycheck), any amount of money you can save in taxes just means more money for your future. As intimidating as tax issues may seem (I feel the same way!), it doesn't mean you have to figure things out all by yourself. The best way forward is to collaborate with your advisor and ask questions through whatever fear you may experience—and that's called courage. By sharing your tax information with your advisor and CPA, you automatically have people in your corner who understand all the potential things that can be done.

It may feel like you have a nasty, scary monster hiding under your bed. Your financial advisor will be the one to lift the sheets and look under there, showing nothing but a pair of slippers and some dust bunnies. That's a tremendous relief.

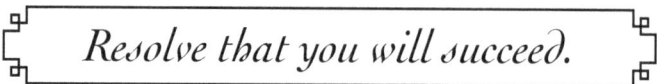

Resolve that you will succeed.

MOST IMPORTANT TAKEAWAYS

1. Required Minimum Distributions (RMDs) start the year following the year you turn seventy-three.

2. Unpaid RMDs carry a 25 percent penalty. But if you did miss it the first time, ask your planner or CPA to assist you in writing the IRS. They will often waive the penalty the first time but won't be so generous the next.

3. Income gaps can be opportunities to begin reducing your future RMD tax bill, but you need to be thinking about this in your late fifties and early sixties. Prepare.

NEXT STEPS

1. Ask your advisor what the plan is for RMD tax savings and find out if the advisor's firm partners with a CPA. If that firm can't give you sound direction on RMDs, you may have outgrown your advisor and should consider working with someone who specializes in retirement planning. You may have multiple accounts, and these will need precise care, balance, and timing. This will likely be one of the most time-consuming parts of your retirement planning process. Make sure you get the appropriate help you need because there are many moving parts. This is your life and your retirement!

2. Consider setting up an automated RMD. This way, you always know it pays on time, the IRS is satisfied, and you might have a time of year where an influx of money would be helpful for you.

3. Go online and look up the top ten questions to ask your financial advisor CPA about taxes, RMDs, and so forth. You do not need to read the 250-page tax code—it's complicated. Familiarize yourself

with the basics of this topic so that you will feel stronger when talking with your professional.

CHAPTER 10

LONGEVITY & HEALTHCARE

> *Current discipline or future regret.*
> *The choice is yours.*

HOW MANY PAP SMEARS?

There's one commonality with most college students—they're usually broke. I was no exception.

After giving up my full-ride scholarships to follow my boyfriend to the University of Washington, I didn't have time to get a job because Division I volleyball required a five-hour commitment each day. Our conditioning workouts lasted from 5:30 to 7 AM. We practiced from 2:30 to 5:30 PM and between those sessions, we attended class. From

6 to 8 PM, we participated in a mandatory study hall. Doesn't that sound like a party?

When I was approached as a freshman to join a cancer study that paid $10 every quarter and included free checkups, I jumped at the chance and didn't ask many questions.

I was one of five hundred freshmen women who agreed to participate in this study. UW hoped to determine the precursor for cervical cancer, a noble aim I barely registered, as I just wanted the cash.

Once I committed to the study, I went to my first appointment and learned the protocol. For the next four years, I agreed to participate in four visits each year and was paid $10 for each visit (by today's inflation, purchasing power of $23). Each required an hour for me to go to the hospital, divulge my private information to a gynecologist, and have two blood draws, a pelvic exam, and *six* pap smears! What did I get myself into? It quickly became apparent that this four-year commitment was not worth the measly compensation.

But I'm not a quitter.

Two years and eight appointments in, the research yielded such significant results that UW received another large grant to continue the study and add another five hundred girls. Program administrators asked the first group to remain in the study for a few additional years.

In the end, I participated for ten years! My commitment to engage in sixteen appointments grew to twenty-eight. By the time the ten years had passed, eighty-seven women from the initial five hundred remained.

Remarkable.

But the most incredible part of that experience for me came twenty-five years after I had first signed up.

I took my middle son, Ashton, in for his twelve-year-old check-up. The doctor checked over his vaccination records and then asked if I wanted him to receive the HPV vaccine. The HPV vaccine helps protect against certain types of viruses that can lead to cancer, particularly cervical cancer. The vaccine, the doctor explained, was developed with research from a study the University of Washington. It began twenty-five years before, with five hundred naïve (broke) freshman girls—*including me.*

Committing to that study in college was not an act of love, but desperation. I needed the cash. After my first visit, though, I had two choices—be a woman of commitment or quit because it was inconvenient and very uncomfortable. All three of my boys, and their future wives, will benefit because eight-seven women, including myself, didn't quit.

I know you are just like me. You don't quit when things get tough or inconvenient.

In the area of health and healthcare, there is a lot to be said about commitment. I am proud to have been a part of such a groundbreaking study that has increased the longevity of so many during my lifetime. While living longer has great benefits, as it relates to your retirement, longevity has the potential to be the biggest risk you face, more than market risk, taxes, or inflation. In the past 125 years, a woman's life expectancy has increased from forty-nine[31] to eighty-one[32]. That's a good thing, but we need to plan for it.

Retirement, as we know it, didn't exist 125 years ago. If you were alive, you worked.

MEDICARE COST-SHIFTING

Longevity runs in Randy's family. His great aunt Louise lived till ninety-one. Her brother, great Uncle Dan, lived till ninety-six, and their oldest sister, Randy's grandmother Agnes, lived to a few months shy of her 101st birthday! Those were all on his mom's side. His dad's mother, Olive, also lived to ninety-seven.

---

31 https://www.health.harvard.edu/blog/why-life-expectancy-in-the-us-is-falling-202210202835#:~:text=With%20rare%20exceptions%2C%20life%20expectancy,year%20span%20since%20the%201920s.
32 https://www.ssb.no/270434/life-expectancy-at-birth.first-year-estimated-then-projected-in-three-alternatives-to-2100

Having started in the retirement planning business in the late eighties, Randy was intimately aware and often involved in the discussions regarding the healthcare of those wonderful family members, since neither Dan nor Louise had children of their own. What he saw regarding Medicare coverage in the early nineties versus what it covered when Grandma Agnes passed in 2013 was vastly different.

He saw firsthand that Medicare shielded the family from much of the dramatic burden of Olive's care, when she battled through Alzheimer's for nearly seven years. Certainly, the family wished it would have covered more, since her long-term care policy eventually ran dry, but Medicare did pick up a large portion of that financial drain.

As Louise, Dan, and Agnes continued to age, as well as Randy's father, John, Randy became increasingly aware that Medicare was not covering many of the costs associated with their care as it had with Olive, decades before. Medicare had largely shifted the burden for their care back to them, personally.

That's frightening.

We need to take personal responsibility for our healthcare planning, because the system won't cover it all. Even if Congress makes miraculous strides to improve our social programs and the economy cooperates, there will be significant changes. There's simply no way, with our growing population and increasing longevity, that we will be able to rely solely on the government to take care of us in our latter years. It may help as a supplement, but we need to be prepared with a plan that includes healthcare management.

The consequences of this are very real in terms of dollars and cents: one estimate says a couple, age sixty-five, in average health, can expect to spend $285,000 on expenses related to healthcare in retirement[33]. Basic medical care, as well as long term care, can drain your savings at an alarming rate if no protection plan is in place.

---

33 Lake, Rebecca. "How to Plan for Medical Expenses in Retirement." Investopedia, December 30, 2022. https://www.investopedia.com/retirement/how-plan-medical-expenses-retirement/

INVESTMENTS ARE NOT A "LIFE" PLAN

When you begin to look toward retirement, you don't need just a mix of stocks, bonds, annuities, and mutual funds—you need a soundly constructed, holistic plan. How will your plan pay for future healthcare should you need it for yourself or your spouse? How will your retirement assets cover future healthcare, especially if you don't have any children that could or would bear that burden if the money ran out?

Educating yourself on the options is vital, and you'll want to work with a professional who can help you understand not only *what* to do but *why* it is so important. I became a financial advisor determined to help women prepare a life plan. With my fire sufficiently ignited to assist the under-served half of our national community—women—I know it is never too late to become who you want to be, to realize who God created you to be, and to feel safe in the process.

You deserve to live your best life and you deserve to feel great and live well. Being proactive about our health flows into every area of our lives, and we are responsible for getting the help that we need.

"A woman's health is her capital." – HARRIET BEECHER STOWE

HEALTHCARE VERSUS SELF-CARE

Don't devalue the seed. A twenty-minute walk can do wonders for your health and mind and doesn't cost a thing. If you do the little things along the way to care for yourself, it means that you will have less drain on your assets in retirement. Caring for your health is one of the best ways to guard your assets in retirement, hands down. It is all about consistency in your self-care and in your finances, not drastic changes that don't last.

There is a saying: "People often spend their health trying to gain wealth, then spend their wealth trying to regain their health." Don't wait to practice self-care—this is the only body you've got.

If money is coming out of your retirement assets to cover healthcare of some sort, I would rather you spend money on pedicures, a personal trainer, a nutritionist, or a massage therapist, rather than on doctors' visits, medication, and devices for mobility assistance. I am grateful to have doctors and medical advancements that help us with our longevity, but each of us bear responsibility for our individual quality of life.

GOOD NUTRITION IS VITAL FOR LONGEVITY

I began working with a nutritionist for the first time, nearing my fifties. I have been an athlete my entire life, but I never once took a focused look, with a specialist, on optimal nutrition for a woman my age. I was shocked at how much jumbled information I had absorbed, and how much of it was completely outdated or no longer applicable for a woman (who is also perimenopausal—*hello hormonal changes!*). My cholesterol was high, and I was struggling at maintaining my fitness and strength, while aches and pains were escalating. I knew I was outmatched to tackle these issues on my own. Within five months, and only four appointments, the direction the nutritionist gave me (linked with my willingness *to do the work)*, dropped my cholesterol forty-nine points, back to where it had been ten years prior!

I thought I was doing enough, yet being an athlete (now an endurance athlete), I realized that an active life did not make me proficient on health and nutrition. Being good with exercise or sports does not mean you know about your internal health. Nutrition is a massive component of our overall self-care (dare I say *the* most important), and it affects everything, including our energy, our recovery, our sleep, *and* our money. The more I spent on high-quality food and supplements going into my mouth and body, the less I spent on areas of medication, doctors' visits, and injury recovery.

Better, nutrient-dense foods kept me satiated longer and I was less likely to reach for the junk food that ran through me like water. The cycle is self-perpetuating. With family history of type 2 diabetes, obesity, joint pain, and cancer, I could not sit back and just let my health decline without putting up a fight. I needed to add effort in this area and become educated. I needed to hire a professional to help me succeed (are you catching the theme here?).

Genetics only account for as much as 25 percent of your longevity[34]; most of it is how you treat the one vessel (the precious body) you have.

YOU DESERVE IT

Consistency is key. Self-care is vital. A massage (or pedicure) is not a luxury you only deserve on your birthday or on a cruise, it is investing in your mental, physical, and emotional well-being. I made that mistake for well over a decade, telling myself it was too expensive or that I didn't deserve that "indulgence." Then one day I realized I was worth a monthly massage, and that the experience made me a better human to everyone around me. It may not be that for you, but what about getting someone in to help with house cleaning or landscaping, so that you can spend that time playing with your grand kids, instead? An advisor can add those items into your plan and show you that those acts of loving yourself will not derail your long-term plan, but enhance your quality of life.

When you feel better, you think better. You *are bett*er.

I want your life to be enjoyable, even when doctors' visits come. A great plan can help you prepare for any necessary major medical interventions, and it can provide for enough money to spend on

---

34 https://medlineplus.gov/genetics/understanding/traits/longevity/#:~:text=The%20study%20of%20longevity%20genes,longevity%2C%20are%20not%20well%20understood

activities that help maintain your mental and physical health. Living better is the best kind of prevention, so that you might avoid many of those major medical events in the first place.

Healthcare is a lifestyle, not a check-off list. It's not the prescriptions you take, nor the fad diet you start after New Year's. It means fresh air, stress management, quality relationships, plenty of sleep, stretching, time for prayer and meditation, lots of water, limiting or eliminating alcohol (too much is costly to your wallet and health), reading meaningful and insightful books, nutritious and delicious meals, and regular preventative measures. It means going to the doctor for check-ups *before* there is a big problem, and making strides forward instead of excuses to stay in the same place. Most of all, self-care is realizing that *you are not alone!*

You have likely had to handle things before. Maybe it was the family finances. Perhaps it was a work issue. Take the same approach to your well-being and health and *handle it*.

INFLATION—THE BOOGEYMAN

If longevity is the biggest risk you face in retirement, inflation is the *sidekick* that often lurks in the shadows right behind. Since 1925, inflation has averaged 2.9 percent[35]. Since women tend to live longer than their male counterparts, inflation will be more impactful to a woman's retirement. Inflation erodes your future purchasing power. If you have $500,000 today, more than thirty years of inflation, at 3 percent on average, will reduce that $500,000 to the purchasing power of $200,000. So, your money doesn't go as far. Healthcare often inflates at an even quicker pace than the average cost of goods and services, creating a double whammy.

You can't avoid inflation by ignoring it.

---

35 Federal Reserve Bank of Minneapolis, "Consumer Price Index, 1913—." https://www.minneapolisfed.org/about-us/monetary-policy/inflation-calculator/consumer-price-index-1913-

Your retirement plan needs inflation factored in to make sure it doesn't derail the future coverage you may need. A comprehensive plan will show you how inflation could affect you long-term.

KIDNEY FAILURE—OR A BROKEN HEART

Met.in.africa.123@aol.com was the couple's email address. They were two of the most vibrant people I've ever met, and they were truly in love with each other! She was a widow from Denmark and he was a widower from the U.S. Neither expected to remarry, but they met by happenstance during a trip to Africa and fell in love. Love has a way of finding you where you least expect it.

By the time Paul and Karen came in seeking our help for their retirement, he was seventy-two and she was sixty-one. They were eleven years apart, just like Randy and me. The age difference endeared them to us even more. Paul was receiving daily kidney dialysis but was handling it reasonably well. Karen, on the other hand, was in exceptional health, and by all statistical accounts she would outlive her husband, possibly by many years, maybe two decades.

Since they came in to seek our help when he was already receiving dialysis, there wasn't a lot of healthcare planning that we could do for him personally, but we wanted to create a plan for Karen. However, they both assumed she wouldn't need a healthcare plan because of her great health (an assumption many people make), so they decided against using some of their assets to create a formal long-term healthcare plan.

- Seven out of ten people will need to receive some form of long-term/nursing home care[36].
- 79 percent of employed Americans plan to continue working for wages in retirement, but only 34 percent actually do. Health-

---

36 https://www.singlecare.com/blog/news/long-term-care-statistics/#:~:text=What%20percentage%20of%20people%20receive,term%20care%20during%20their%20lifetime.

related issues are one of the primary factors that force them out of the work force before they had planned[37].

Paul and Karen decided to self-fund any future needs, and they continued their active and energetic life.

Until the day Karen fell.

She had such a major head injury that the next time we saw her, a few months later, she was wheelchair-bound. Her vivacity had all but vanished. Paul was doing his best to keep his spirits up, and hers as well. It was increasingly difficult to retain a smile as he attempted to care for her in his own physically compromised state. Within a couple of months, he came to the brutal realization that she needed full-time care, yet the assets they had were not enough to cover in-home care for the exhaustive nature of what she was now facing.

Paul needed outside help desperately.

Karen's children stepped in, as we often see in situations like these. Most women do not want to be a burden on their children. This is a throughline with most the women I meet. Yet a daughter will rise to the occasion more often than not and assume the role as caregiver. Karen's daughter was no different. She saw the need her mother had, and she handled it. She suggested that her mom move in with her, and Paul reluctantly and achingly agreed. He knew that was the best option for his wife.

One day in the fall of 2007, he drove his wife to SeaTac Airport and put her on a plane to head back to Denmark to receive care from her family.

...without him.

Because of his daily need for dialysis, Paul had to stay behind. He recognized that day was the last day he would kiss her lips or hold her hand.

---

[37] Modglin, Lindsay. "Long Term Care Statistics 2022." The Checkup by Singlecare, December 15, 2022. https://www.singlecare.com/blog/news/long-term-care-statistics/#:~:text=What%20percentage%20of%20people%20receive,term%20care%20during%20their%20lifetime.

The next two visits we had with Paul were absolutely gut-wrenching. Here was a seventy-year-old man sobbing in our office because he had lost his best friend. Because of her condition, even video conferencing via Skype or FaceTime was not a very effective way to stay in touch. He had lost his second wife, not by death, but by distance. Within six months of putting her on the plane, Paul passed away from kidney failure coupled with a broken heart.

The most difficult part about that experience, for us as planners, was that Paul and Karen had enough assets that they could have provided a level of support at home, had they approved the measures we suggested before Karen's accident. *The time to act is now;* don't wait until it's too late.

LIKE CAR INSURANCE

Many people can't stand the thought of traditional long-term care insurance because it reminds them of car insurance. You pay these premiums for an unknown period, and then if you don't need that type of care, all that money's *gone*. As I've said multiple times, having control and options in retirement is paramount. I'm not a huge fan of traditional long-term care. It typically begins to get more expensive as the years progress, but there are suitable alternatives.

BETTER OPTIONS THAT RETAIN CONTROL

Often, we may look at *asset-based long-term care* or a *home healthcare doubler* added to an annuity.

Asset-based long-term care is an option for reasonably healthy people in their forties and fifties, and possibly early sixties. This means that you can take a chunk of assets, say for example $50,000, give it to an insurance company to purchase an annuity with an added long-term care rider (included at an additional annual cost), and if you meet certain conditions outlined in the annuity, it will provide you added funds to pay for assisted living or nursing home coverage. The annuity typically multiplies your regular income benefit by a certain amount, such as three or four times, up to a defined period, such as three to five years. If you were to die and never use the policy, the annuity's remaining value would distribute to your assigned beneficiaries rather than staying in the insurance company's pocket.

However, one constant I have seen all these years is that people change their minds. Down the road, if you have another idea and want to cancel your annuity to put a down payment on a condo in Arizona (or something else fun), the insurance company often lets you add a feature that ensures you get your premium back. The insurance industry calls this a *guaranteed return of premium* (ROP) option, and you may pay an added cost for this each year. Some companies provide 100 percent ROP on day one, and others graduate it over five to seven years. Either way, it is refreshing to have options and exit strategies because no one can predict the future.

Another option is a *fixed index annuity* with a *home healthcare doubler* attached to the income rider. Sometimes the rider includes a fee, and sometimes it is included as a standard benefit. With this rider, if you need care—if you can no longer perform two of six activities of daily living (ADLs)—and your annuity usually pays out, for example, $2,500, activating this rider means the insurance will double that amount to $5,000 per month for a set period, say three years. Every policy is different, and it is necessary to understand what the best option is for you by seeing it in conjunction with your entire retirement plan. The bottom line is that there are new and refreshing alternatives to the often oppressive and unpredictable aspects of traditional long-term care policies.

You owe it to yourself to explore these opportunities. I'll bet you didn't even know you had options!

SHOULD I SCRAP MY CURRENT LTC POLICY?

If you have a traditional long-term care insurance policy, but you don't have a comprehensive retirement plan, you have a "microclimate" for long-term care. You may be asking yourself whether you should continue payments on that traditional policy, especially if you receive frequent premium increases. Until you see how it looks in the context of the entire plan, you can't answer that. Some people find the premiums to be such a drain on their fixed income, it becomes too expensive to own. Other people are right in a sweet spot.

Sit down with your advisor and see how your current long-term care coverage functions within the overall picture of your retirement plan before you make the drastic decision to drop your coverage. Be careful about deleting something you may not be able to replace. While you are discussing these plans with your financial professional, please be sure to have conversations with your family members, so they know how to support you and organize for the future. Your health and well-being affect everyone, and it is important for your entire family understand their role in your plans.

FINDING YOUR HAPPY PLACE

The most essential lesson is how you take care of yourself along the way. Yes, this means your heart health, your blood pressure, and your vitamins, but self-care is actually reaches farther than "the self." Your life is also the life of your spouse, your children, your friends, and your family, so take please consider how your decisions and habits affect those who love you. Good health is balance, mindfulness, and living with a purpose, and these are qualities we can all share in together. You will set the pace in positive self-care, and show the next generations how proper living is done! Loving yourself is part of your legacy!

I've heard it said that *self-care is giving the very best of you, instead of what's left of you.*

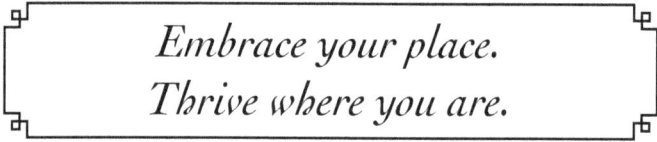

*Embrace your place.
Thrive where you are.*

MOST IMPORTANT TAKEAWAYS

1. Longevity is one of the most significant risks you face, often more than market risk, taxes or inflation.

2. Right now, the largest amount of cost-shifting in history is happening with things that used to be covered by Medicare.

3. One estimation anticipates that a couple, age sixty-five, average health, is expected to spend $315,000 on health-care-related expenses through their retirement, and that figure increased 5 percent from just the year before[38].

4. People often spend their health trying to gain wealth, then spend their wealth trying to regain their health. Spend more of your money on healthy activities that keep you well to lessen the drain on your assets for future medical intervention.

---

[38] https://www.cnbc.com/2022/05/16/americans-can-expect-to-pay-a-lot-more-for-medical-care-in-retirement.html

5. Genetics account for only 25 percent of your longevity. The greatest impact is how you treat your body[39].
6. Seven out of ten adults will need some form of long-term care[40]. Plan accordingly.

NEXT STEPS

1. Be sure to add a little extra expense to your financial plan every month for activities that enhance your health (i.e., pedicure, massage, therapist, nutritionist) and bring you joy.

2. Be willing to look squarely at how the cost of long-term care may derail your retirement plan. This should be a specific discussion with your planner. For married women, this is vastly important to your overall financial security and peace of mind following your spouse's death.

3. If you are in your forties and fifties, this is a good time to look at long-term care funding options with your planner. Your health may never be better than it is today. Consider that it may be more price advantageous to look at these options sooner rather than later.

4. Ask about *asset-based long-term care* or *home healthcare doublers* on annuity contracts as alternative options to traditional long-term care insurance.

---

[39] https://medlineplus.gov/genetics/understanding/traits/longevity/#:~:text=The%20study%20of%20longevity%20genes,longevity%2C%20are%20not%20well%20understood.
[40] "2020 Census Will Help Policymakers Prepare for the Incoming Wave of Aging Boomers", site accessed 01/10/22.

CHAPTER 11

PROTECTION FOR THE UNEXPECTED

> *Stop flailing, slowly inhale, then take one step toward your destiny.*

110 POUNDS OF VISCERAL FORCE

One of the highlights of my role as Assistant Clinic Director of Sarvey Wildlife Care Center was getting *loved on* by a 110-pound cougar named Sasha. A tawny brown color, Sasha was soft, stunning, playful, and powerful.

An interesting fact about cougars: they are the largest of the *small* cats, meaning they are more closely related to a domestic cat than they are to a lion or tiger. *One primary distinction is* that they can purr. Big cats cannot. Can you imagine the deep, wonderful purr of a cat that size? It was intoxicating; you could feel it deep within your chest.

Sasha was one of our permanent residents. Someone bought her legally from a breeder in Texas, but then illegally brought her to Washington State as a cub. By the time she was a juvenile at the age of eighteen months, she was too much for the owner to handle. Only four people who worked at Sarvey could handle her. I was one of the lucky four.

Every day when she would hear me walking down the path, she would catcall to me. A massive cat "chirping" to me with excitement was a thrill. Her purr would kick in the moment she heard my catcall back to her. It was a wonderful bond. Because of her trust in me and the relationship I built over many years, I oversaw cleaning her enclosure, changing her water, and removing her half-eaten carcasses. But the ultimate joy I experienced was playing games with her.

Many of the times that I went in with Sasha, I would bring a large rope toy, the kind you would use to play tug-of-war with a German Shepard or Retriever. We would use it the same way. Sasha would lie on the ground, and she would play with this big rope, as if I was teasing an overgrown house cat. It was a blast!

One warm summer day, Judy, one of our volunteers, asked if she could come in with me and take photos of Sasha while we were playing tug-o-war. It seemed like a great day for it, so I agreed.

Judy and I made our way in through the first chain-linked door to the holding area, part of a double-door of security, just in case Sasha ever made it through the first door. We got all the things ready that we were bringing in, in addition to the rope to play tug-o-war. As the first door locked behind us, I opened the second, and we made our way into Sasha's enclosure.

Sasha cat-called to me from her perch, purring like we were long-lost pals. As I continued in, she jumped down and came up to rub the scent glands on the side of her cheeks on my pant leg. Judy entered the pen, closed the second chain-linked door behind her and prepared her camera. In an instant, Sasha's body tensed, her ears laid flat back against her head, and she was bearing her two-inch canines.

Something had changed.

Sasha swung her mouth around to bite down hard on my right thigh. The force and power she wielded was shocking. Before I could get my bearings, Sasha let go of my right leg and jumped up to wrap her massive and powerful front paws around my waist, sinking her razor-sharp teeth into the left side of my chest, then immediately into the right.

Judy began to scream as I tried to regain control of this apex predator that weighed only 15 pounds less than me. Sasha then dropped back to all fours before clamping down onto my only non-bitten appendage, my left thigh. Judy was in a total panic, and I was terrified Sasha would go for her.

I was utterly shocked at how fast it went from bad to worse, awed by the sheer flexibility and speed of a cat like that. If not for her declawed front paws, I would have been vastly outmatched that day.

Still shrieking, Judy escaped the enclosure, leaving me to defend myself (thanks a lot Judy!). I shoved my left hand into Sasha's mouth, grabbed her throat with my right hand, and kneed her forcefully in the chest. She moaned, and finally let go, allowing me to leave.

Having heard the first chain-linked door close behind me, I took stock of my injuries. But just as soon as I had exited, Sasha was back up to the side of the enclosure purring as if we were long lost friends, as though nothing had happened. I've had domestic cats all my life, and it was reminiscent of their bizarre behaviors. One moment they are relaxed and happy to be caressed and loved, and the next, their teeth are sinking into your palm while their back legs claw your skin. Domesticated or wild, they have a perplexing nature.

PLANNING FOR THE UNEXPECTED, THE UNKNOWN

Severe maiming was not part of my story that day, but it wasn't due to luck. Avoiding serious injury was the result of planning and preparation for the unknown, for the unexpected. I received major pressure wounds on both sides of my chest and thighs, but nothing broke the surface, thank God, because I had the right protection for the job.

It was an 85-degree day in July, but I was still wearing full-length jeans, a long-sleeved t-shirt, hoodie sweatshirt, and a heavy Levi denim jacket with wool lining on the inside. When you work with wild animals, you don't leave anything to chance.

If Sasha had wanted to really hurt me, she would have chomped down on my hand, breaking every bone in it. That was never her intention. She loved me, but deep down she was still wild and there was something about Judy's presence that set her off. This wonderfully confused animal was torn between her survival instincts and wanting to be touched, played with, and petted. Yet I knew Sasha was wild down to her bones and must never to be taken for granted, so I always went in properly prepared. And for those wondering, Sasha and I remained great pals in the remaining years that I worked at Sarvey.

COOL, CALM AND COLLECTED

Life is full of frightening and unexpected situations. We may get bad news, have an accident, suffer a loss, or go through a tragic emergency, but what really makes the difference is *how we react.* Our heart may be racing in a full-fledged panic, but that doesn't mean that it has to be a worst-case scenario. We need to be prepared. I was of course afraid in those moments with Sasha—fight or flight—but I didn't lose my focus. I knew how to react because I had been trained, had protective attire, and inherently knew she wasn't going to kill me.

It was a lesson in feeling the fear and riding the wave without overreacting, because responding with terror would have only made the situation worse. Imagine if I had gone into the cage in a tank top and shorts, or if I had not faced her head-on and with my own power, confidence, and authority? How we handle life in the moment depends on how well we are prepared and if we can face down the fear with courage.

If you are heading into a recession or a major market downturn and you don't have a comprehensive plan, an advisor, and a long-term perspective, you are likely going to have some achingly sleepless nights. Market fluctuations are normal, and having a well-managed portfolio with someone you can trust and talk to will get you through those "now what?!" recession-like moments. Remember that the market changes regularly, but things *always* come back. Fluctuations are normal, and you can plan for them. Hang in there: you've got this, and you are not alone. With a smart system in place, you won't have those panic attacks that urge you to make desperate decisions you might regret.

When life comes at you like an angry cougar, you can be prepared and make it through with minimal harm. You may suffer minor discomfort, but you will recover, and the right advisor and mentor will walk you each step of the way.

PROTECTING WHAT MATTERS MOST—WHITE PICKET FENCE

Most people think life insurance, even the cheapest kind (term insurance), is only for those who have young kids or a mortgage. In many minds, it acts as the white picket fence standing around those things and people that matter most.

That's not untrue, but life insurance can also be a lot more.

Insurance is, at its foundation, always going to be about the death benefit. But there are now some very sophisticated products that also provide benefits like cash savings, tax strategies, charitable giving opportunities, long-term care funding, and on and on. Great advisors integrate these different kinds of policies within the broad context of an overall plan to provide advantages and protection for clients.

One commonality is that insurance costs and policy lengths always vary based on the insured's health, a factor that can change rapidly and alter or eliminate your chances of coverage. That's why it's incredibly important to have this conversation with your financial planner sooner rather than later. Remember, lack of planning is still a plan.

CHEAP IS NOT ALWAYS A BAD THING

You may benefit from an inexpensive ten- or twenty-year term insurance policy on your spouse. If they die prematurely, that kind of policy can ensure that you have proper assets to last the rest of your life. The premium never goes up, but, like car insurance, should that person outlive that time period, those premiums are gone for good. Not ideal, but still better than if they die prematurely and you are left with insufficient resources. When you meet with your advisor, it is important that they show what it might look like if your spouse died early in retirement (or before you retire) and if you would have enough money to pay the mortgage or put your children through college.

This was a huge piece of mind for me in my thirties and forties when we had to dig out of our big financial hole, yet we had a mortgage, three kids and a business to still run. This gave me some security that if something happened to either Randy or me, our family would be able to stay in our home, have their needs met, and exhale for a bit as they recovered from a tremendous loss of mom or dad. Thankfully we never needed to use the policy, but the small minimal monthly outlay gave me great comfort. It might do the same for you. Ask about it.

If you are single, the same may apply for the protection of your heirs. Life insurance may provide the ability to handle the settling of your estate slowly and systematically upon your passing. This is far more advantageous than heirs rushing to sell your home or liquidating IRAs to pay your tax bill within the allotted nine months required. Many kids must hurry to sell their parents' house, which puts a ton of pressure on them to get it emptied and ready to sell. The market may not be in the best position to facilitate a favorable sale. It's also hard to pack up and sell a house when you are sad. In times of grief, the last thing a family member wants to do is legal work or real estate. They just want time to grieve.

Life insurance proceeds give beneficiaries tax-free money to pay tax bills and final expenses for funerals and memorials. Such proceeds allow them time to mourn instead of immediately having to confront a financial calamity while grieving. I am not saying that you have created a situation like that, but you must openly discuss what your death will mean for your heirs or how, if you are married, your spouse's death will impact you.

WHO'S PREPARED FOR ANOTHER GREAT RECESSION OR BLACK SWAN EVENT?

Me! If you can't say that, the question back would be, "Why not?"

Having learned several tough financial lessons as we traveled through 2008 and the years directly following, Randy and I decided we were not going to make those same mistakes again. We were determined to be ready in case of another difficult financial time. We were going to eliminate all debt outside of our mortgage. We were going to have adequate life insurance and fully fund our retirement plans. We were going to start paying ourselves first instead of pouring 100 percent of our revenue back into our business. We were going to have six months of personal emergency reserves. We were going to fully fund our boys' college plans and teach them financial basics and about managing money. We were going to give generously when we felt compelled. We were going to make sure we were financially healthy for anything that came our way.

That was a tall order, and it took years, but we did it.

Pain is a great teacher, and when the COVID-19 shutdowns of March 2020 hit, we were extremely healthy because we had learned from and applied the lessons we had endured. We kept all fourteen of our full-time staff employed, and we had a record business year even though 80 percent of our marketing came through dinner seminars (and, in Washington State, they would not let us gather for nineteen months). We had no idea that a pandemic was coming (and who did?), but we got our business and personal finances into a space where we weren't relying on credit, the next sale, or anyone else. We were thriving, and that ricocheted through us to our employees, who helped us dig deep, get creative, weather the storm, and support our clients through the craziness of a worldwide pandemic. It is one of my proudest moments as a business owner (and wife of the other co-owner who lead the charge with conviction and confidence)!

Being prepared and self-assured feels much better than worrying and flailing! Our key to security was to take responsibility, which meant not just having goals and good ideas, but doing the hard work to make them happen. Great planning is not hard to do, but you need help from those who have gone before you and walked that path. Furthermore, you need to know the proper *attire* to protect yourself, in the form of solid planning that looks closely at market risk (Chapter Eight) and how much you could lose in another major market decline.

Whether it's a global pandemic, a market meltdown, a personal emergency, or a defensive mountain lion cornering you, know that these things happen. Life is an adventure. There's likely another one just around the bend. How will you fare? The good news is that you can be just fine, starting today!

Healthcare, market risk, and longevity are the three biggest what-ifs in retirement. Make sure you have clear answers to all of these. Your loved ones will be forever grateful for your foresight.

> *Consistency is the driving factor that dictates the trajectory of your life.*

MOST IMPORTANT TAKEAWAYS

1. Hope for the best but plan for the worst.

2. Lack of planning is a plan…a foolish one. Don't procrastinate.

3. Insurance may be a strong addition to your legacy for your heirs and allow them to take the time needed to grieve, instead of doing asset liquidation to pay the bills your death created.

4. Inexpensive term insurance may give you the assurance that you need to walk through the next twenty years with your new spouse, home, kids, etc.

NEXT STEPS

1. Ask your advisor to show you what your retirement plan looks like if your spouse dies prematurely. You should be able to see if that causes you to run out of money before age 100.

2. Health dictates whether you can qualify for most insurance, so you need to confront this shortly after your team has devised your retirement plan. At your next appointment, ask your advisor to show you if insurance would be of benefit and start "shopping" for it while your health is still good.

3. Get educated on the different types of insurance offered and how they may benefit you and your family.

4. Communicate your ideas and plans with your spouse and family. Don't just tell that *what* you have planned, but *why*.

CHAPTER 12

WHY HIRE AN ADVISOR?

> *The separation is in the preparation; get to work.*

THE ARTIST AND THE ENGINEER

When Earnest and Laura came into our office, our appointment began with an out-of-the-ordinary greeting. Laura saw me, got all giddy and excited like I was a celebrity, hugged me tight, and told me how excited she was to be in our office. I ushered them into the conference room where our yummy treat plate waited on the table. After a few moments of pleasantries, she sat down at the table and said directly to me, "He handles everything." She then proceeded to stare off in the distance out the window.

Uh, okay, I thought.

Her husband walked in and sat down beside her. As I made my way around the table to sit down across from them and initiated small talk, but he launched right in and said, "I have nearly $500,000 in a 401(k) still at my former employer. I want to talk about investing it in a fixed index annuity." I was taken aback by how direct he was, though most financial advisors would instantly have jumped in to address the specifics of his request.

But to his slight frustration and disappointment, I didn't.

"You know, I apologize, Earnest, but I really need to ask some questions before we get into any of that discussion. To be honest with you, we won't discuss that specifically in this visit and probably won't get into that at the next visit, either," I said. "It's important for me, as a fiduciary, to make sure I'm doing what's best for you, and it's also very important for the protection of my licensure to make sure that I'm giving the proper recommendation based on your specific situation. That would be like you going to the doctor and telling them in the first thirty seconds that you want them to prescribe Percocet before they've looked over your medical records or done a physical. That can get me in a whole lot of trouble." I smiled.

He smiled back and nodded in agreement.

"It's important that I look at your overall financial picture and how it all functions together before I make that recommendation." I then looked over at Laura, who was still staring out the window, and said, "but I think that will also be really helpful for you." I pointed to his wife and looked her right in the eyes. She looked startled, with a look on her face that expressed, "I can't believe she's talking to me!"

Yep, I am talking to you, too. Your opinions and thoughts matter!

We spoke about their concerns and why they wanted to meet with us, shared our planning philosophy, and cited our perspective on how to get things done. As usual, moving through a dialogue of the prospective client's values and ideas of a good life and retirement, we'd conclude by working through a general understanding of their current financial and life situation.

If the advisor you are interviewing begins with a discussion about your financials, that will tell you a lot about how they work. They are more focused on your money than they are on you. It's vital to find someone who wants a long-term transformational relationship, not a transactional one, so have your antenna up high in this first meeting.

OPENING THE FLOODGATES

As we began to talk about what was on Earnest's mind (other than the 401(k) at his former employer), he really didn't have much to discuss.

"What about you, Laura? Is there anything that you are concerned about regarding your retirement or current financial picture?" She smiled and shook her head. I asked a few more probing questions, but something special happened when I asked about the long-term health. That opened the floodgates.

"Everyone in your family dies before they reach seventy. You're sixty-eight!" Laura leveled at Earnest.

"My last physical was fine," he responded.

"You don't eat well," Laura quipped.

"I'm healthy as an ox," Earnest pushed back.

Their banter became rather comical, but it was clear they were reaching the heart of a chasm in their communication—a void that had gone unfilled for years. Earnest was a great provider, yet emotionally disconnected from the needs of his wife. He had worked hard to care for his family in the best way he knew how, and had largely succeeded. Yet, when Laura hinted at her deep and growing fear of being left alone and exposed, he was quick to say, "Honey, we are fine, we have enough money."

But his pacifying response to her didn't cut it. It was unfair that he held the reigns, while her passive-aggressive defenses prickled him like barbed wire. He knew their financial picture with his eyes closed, and loved to study and think about it, while she had zero clue.

In black-and-white, she'd never seen any actual evidence to support a resolution to her question, "Will I be okay?" And Earnest wasn't the most qualified to address that in a way that connected with her—as most of us struggle somewhat with the concrete reality of what the world might look like once we are no longer in it. For years, she had been barely keeping a lid on her mounting sense of panic.

From Laura, I could sense a surge of resentment. She did not have an active part in their planning, but she clearly had opinions and desires of how she wanted things to go. I could feel her uneasiness, but I also understood that she had not done her part to understand their situation or educate herself to a degree. Of course, no one had encouraged her to get involved or pushed her to learn more about money. Now, she was waiting (angrily and anxiously), for him to work things out on her behalf. So, yes, they were very well-off, but their communication breakdown did little for her feelings of financial security. What's the use of having money when its benefits remain hidden?

Thus, between them, there was a significant division. He was a detail-oriented engineer who wanted to micro-manage. She just wanted to feel secure, and had never even had access to more than $3,000 at a time to spend as she saw fit—despite the $3 million in wealth they had.

He was focused on the next investment, while she was focused on her future security and safety. Their dynamics were off, and they were facing a looming relationship crisis.

After fifty minutes, we concluded our visit and scheduled a second meeting. I had plenty of information to build a plan showing them where they currently were—*YOU ARE HERE*—and they only needed to supply me with their investment statements from their brokerage accounts. They agreed to get me those in the next few days prior to our next visit. While we were just tackling the tip of the iceberg, I never imagined what was truly going on below the surface.

YOU ARE HERE

A week had passed, and Earnest and Laura were back in the office to see me. We headed back into one of our conference rooms and enjoyed some brief conversation. I asked if anything had changed since we last spoke, then re-read my notes from our initial visit. We were all back on the same page.

I launched our retirement planning software on the TV screen to walk them through the *YOU ARE HERE* picture of their retirement, and when she saw it, her body language changed completely. She sat up straight and tall, turned her entire body to face the TV, and watched intently. Her eyes glowed, and it was like watching an intrigued kid see snow falling for the first time. When we got to the end of it, she pointed at the screen and said loud and directly, "That! That, whatever that is, I want it!" speaking to wanting a printed copy of her comprehensive retirement plan. That was one of the highlight moments of my entire career. At that moment, I saw a disengaged woman realize she could truly understand her financial picture after forty-four years of marriage.

It was awesome!

When she saw that our retirement planning software could distill her entire financial picture in a way she comprehended (without the distractions of the specific technical intricacies that her husband enjoyed), you could see a woman becoming empowered and starting to feel comfortable. She began to pull her head out of the sand and appreciate all her husband had done. All Laura needed was to see the big picture that told her the money they've saved over all these years could be enough to take her through retirement, protect them both through any healthcare events, protect her if he passed away prematurely, and let them live the retirement of their dreams! We spelled it out for her, plain and simple, so that her eyes and heart could finally see.

I looked at her and said, "Well, my dear, spoiler alert: you have more than enough money. By the time you're in your eighties, you should still have a couple million remaining." She had a look of shock on her face, but then her grin quickly distorted and with a bit of a chuckle she quipped, "I don't want to die with all that money!" Then she paused with a glare in her eyes, looked at her husband, then looked back at me and asked, "Then why is he so frugal?" I laughed quietly and said, "Well, that's something you'll have to talk to him about. Maybe that's why you're where you're at financially!"

It was amusing to watch, but it spoke volumes about her lack of understanding of their "big picture."

A PICTURE SHE FINALLY UNDERSTOOD

By the end of the second visit, she had a comprehensive retirement plan that showed her their basic account values and what companies held what. She felt included and she felt heard. We had discussed whether or not they were at risk of running out of money, and how all of their assets could work together with his pension, both of their Social Security benefits, inflation, and taxes. Their investments by themselves, in a micro-climate, didn't tell her that she would be cared for in her eighties if he died and she needed long-term care. That is the purpose of having a written comprehensive plan.

The financial plan we constructed for Laura and Earnest seemed eye-opening, especially for her. When she was holding it in her hands, caressing the edges of the pages between her fingers, you would think that she was cradling filaments of woven gold. She was touching "financial clarity" for the first time with amazement and awe. Laura finally realized the results of her husband's years of work and care for their finances. His years of saving had paid off, and she now felt that she would be taken care of for the rest of her life.

That realization is the huge difference between just "investing" and holistic retirement planning.

> Many people question the value that an advisor brings to your bottom line. The truth is a great advisor can be worth more than 3 percent annually. According to the well-known Vanguard Research Report, the benefit that an advisor can bring can be quite significant.[41] [42]
>
> **LOWER EXPENSE – COST-EFFECTIVE INVESTMENT IMPLEMENTATION = 45 BASIS POINTS (0.45% SAVINGS)**
>
> **REBALANCING – KEEPING YOUR INVESTMENTS ALIGNED = 35 BASIS POINTS (0.35%) SAVINGS**
>
> **BEHAVIOR COACHING – HELPING YOU TO NOT HURT YOURSELF = 150 BASIS POINTS (1.50%) SAVINGS**
>
> **ASSET LOCATION – OPTIMIZING PORTFOLIO THAT MINIMIZES TAXES = 0 TO 75 BASIS POINTS (0.75%) SAVINGS**
>
> **SPENDING STRATEGY – THE WAY YOU WITHDRAW YOUR MONEY = 0 TO 70 BASIS POINTS (0.70%)**
>
> If you add up all of these benefits of your advisor, you can see that comes to 3.75 percent! Let the expert help you prepare and perform better than you can do on your own!

JUST ONE MORE

Most great financial advisors I know will meet with a prospect two to three times before bringing them on as a new client. This is industry

---

41 https://advisors.vanguard.com/insights/article/putting-a-value-on-your-value-quantifying-advisors-alpha#:~:text=Putting%20a%20value%20on%20your%20value%3A%20Quantifying%20Advisor's%20Alpha,-Whitepaper&text=This%20research%20paper%20delves%20into,trying%20to%20outperform%20the%20market.

42 Bach, David. *Smart Women Finish Rich*. Published in the United States by Currency, an imprint of the Crown Publishing Group, a division of Penguin Random House LLC. New York. 1998, 2002, 2018

standard. In our firm, we would generally start working with a new client on the second visit. Sometimes it would take a third. When interviewing advisors, I would shy away from anyone who wants you to sign paperwork in the initial meeting. And, on the flip side, if you are in visit five and beyond and have not yet decided if you want to work with this person, *you* may be the issue. They are not offering non-profit consultation, and their time is valuable; if you don't trust them enough to engage in a relationship with *some* of your money (I didn't say all) by visit four, it may be that you just have trust issues. Consider meeting with a counselor to address some of the deeper confidence issues that prevent you from making a decision. Analysis paralysis is not good for a working relationship.

FINANCIAL GUIDANCE CAN SAVE A MARRIAGE

Earnest and Laura needed a bit more information before continuing the process, so we moved into our third visit. The two arrived separately and, as Earnest and I waited for Laura's arrival, I figured he'd want to launch into the crux of his very first question about fixed index annuities. I prepared my discussion points, but he stopped me.

"Before we get started, I wanted to tell you how grateful I am for what you did for my wife. It meant so much to her to see things the way they were laid out, and it meant a lot to me, too. She left that last meeting so happy." That was a tough thing for an engineer to communicate, but it was a massive turning point in their marriage.

It was remarkable to watch these two grow closer to each other through financial planning. Seeing his wife make the shift from doubt, ignorance, and frustration to clarity and peace of mind (about the future of her security and her marriage) really affected him. The entire experience was a major touchstone in my career. Laura was able to see the first collective snapshot of all that she and her husband had worked for and created. This comprehensive look at their retirement accounts combined all those micro-climates into one, and it made all the difference. Giving people certainty and lucidity is one of the most powerful aspects of being a retirement planner.

But their story didn't end there.

Randy and I have been told over the years that we have saved marriages. Guidance is very much a part of what we do—and not just concerning numbers. The definition of advisor is "a person who gives advice," and counsel was something that Earnest needed desperately. Randy and I did many of our visits as a team, and when we had an individual that wanted to talk through the deep data behind the investments and tools we used, Randy was *the guy*. He was able to go toe-to-toe with any of the smartest engineers regarding personal finance and help them to grasp the complex details. Since that was how Earnest was hardwired, he took a great liking to Randy. They spoke the same language. Earnest really needed wisdom and he knew exactly who to call.

Earnest told us that they were facing a crisis: he had lost $750,000, nearly a third of their retirement assets, in a bad investment Laura knew nothing about. He recognized that the news was going to set his wife back to the place of dread she had just emerged from. Again, he needed Randy's help.

The advice he received was not what he expected. "Earnest, you need to put $100,000 in a bank account that your wife has access to do as she pleases." What? The look on Earnest's face was shock. How was that solving the issue?

He just lost $750,000 and now was being asked to carve out more money for his wife to possibly lose? Earnest had micro-managed (a.k.a. controlled) all the finances for their forty-four-year marriage and had been so frugal that he only deposited $3,000 per month into an account for her use and spending. This perpetuated much of the reason she always felt broke. "But what if she blows it all?" he retorted.

Randy responded: "She may, but most likely she won't spend much of it. It will just give her a feeling of freedom and security to do as she pleases, just as you have. And if she does spend it, which again she likely won't because of the spending habits she already has, it won't damage your long-term picture any more than your $750,000 loss has. She deserves the same level of financial freedom that you enjoy." Wow. Honest advice and a bit shocking to his system, but to Earnest's credit, he left our office and took Randy's advice.

Months later, Laura approached me at our annual client event, "Your husband saved our marriage!" Indeed, Randy served as a thoughtful and caring intermediary who had an eye on finances as well as a heart for their marriage conflict. He helped them work together. Randy understood the husband's business-mind point of view, but was well-aware of the wife's needs for inclusion and independence. In the end, he recommended that she be given her own account, so that she felt genuinely part of the married team—rather than always having to ask for permission.

EVERYONE DESERVES TO FEEL HEARD

A great advisor will be the referee between you and your spouse to help you communicate and define your boundaries. For those of you that are single, they will be the voice of reason that helps you battle the negative and self-defeating thoughts and fears in your own mind. We are all haunted by toxic thoughts of years gone by, and an advisor will help keep you in the present. Before you can plan, you'll want to understand your individual financial love language.

Now is the time to educate yourself and ask questions. There may be a major difference in financial approaches between you and your spouse, and that's quite common. But recognize it. Randy and I found that talking to a marriage therapist was a huge benefit when talking about money, because emotional layers can prevent us from getting things done. Don't take it personally if your spouse has different beliefs or values, or a completely different style. This isn't about being wrong or right—only *different*.

It goes back to a topic discussed in previous chapters—values-based financial planning. There is always a *why*, or a motivation, when choices are made. Sometimes these differences are tangible, and sometimes they are intangible.

For example, I remember one time where I wanted to make an investment in doing a speaker training course. I felt it would bring great value because of the discipline and knowledge I would gain in becoming a better public speaker. It would be a tremendous experience, though it required a significant financial and time commitment. Randy, on the other hand, was interested in spending money to buy a classic guitar. I thought it was a lot of money for an instrument! Other than making music, what would the long-term benefits of such a purchase be? How could he compare my developmental training course to wanting a new guitar? He didn't understand why the experience would be so important to me, but neither did I see the value he had assigned to a classic guitar.

Both would be investments. But it took some explaining to understand why we felt our individual choices were important to us. His was tangible—a thing. Mine was intangible—personal enrichment. The solution wasn't one over the other; we solved the problem by eliminating the actual problem, which was our miscommunication.

BUT I ALREADY HAVE A FINANCIAL ADVISOR

You might even have two or three financial advisors. That's okay. It's common because we go through different seasons of our financial lives. I can vividly recall my first softball coach, volleyball coach, and my first two weightlifting coaches as some of the best mentors in my life. But they could not prepare me for my first half-marathon. They each specialized in other areas of athletic development and that was no longer applicable to the next phase of my athletic career… endurance races.

Your current advisor may specialize in accumulation of wealth: growing, saving, and adjusting to situations people confront in their twenties, thirties, and early forties. But when you start transitioning into your fifties, and beyond, many unique pieces must be addressed for *that* season of life. You want to be talking to somebody who is an independent fiduciary and somebody who specializes in retirement planning, and who can coordinate your finances with tax planning during the years you are no longer working a job.

PEDIATRICIAN AT FIFTY?

If you remain with the advisor who helped you save all your money for the last twenty years, it might be like staying with your childhood pediatrician until you hit age fifty. He or she may be the kindest, friendliest, most world-class medical professional, but they wouldn't be prepared to deal with your questions about menopause or loss of bladder control! I don't care how amazing, nice, skilled, good-looking, or knowledgeable the person is; their area of expertise is treating children. Period.

You need to hire a retirement planner who specializes in helping you protect your assets, income and healthcare planning, risk-managed growth, RMD planning and tax integration. Not only should they be knowledgeable about these areas, but they should be proactive and have a personality and attitude that meshes well with yours—ideally, they will be working with you for a long time. It's not enough to just "have somebody." Don't skimp of quality coaching because you don't want to spend the time or the money—that may lead to real future damage. Retirement is not something you want to compromise on. You deserve the best. This is your one precious life!

Seasons of life change and the coaches you need along the way ought to change along with you.

SAVE ME FROM MY KIDS

"My daughter is mad because I won't give her some money," Linda told me after coming in for a visit. Then, she began to cry.

She mentioned she had just received a final payout for a piece of property that her family had owned; the proceeds were split between her and her ex-husband. She divorced in her early sixties and was now nearing seventy. The $110,000 she received from the sale was going to be exactly what she needed to fulfill the remaining long-term goals of her retirement.

Unfortunately, her daughter also found out about the payment and began to put the hard press on her mom to share. Her daughter was self-sufficient, as one generally ought to be by their mid-forties, but had been quite upset that she hadn't gotten what she saw as *her share*.

Linda was looking for confirmation she did the right thing, even though she felt terrible about it. After we plugged everything into her retirement plan, it showed very clearly that she absolutely needed that money for the overall health of her retirement and future healthcare planning. Shaving off $30,000 or $40,000 of those proceeds would diminish the long-term viability of her plan and her deep sense of peace. She was able to see the negative effect herself as we simulated that "alternate plan," which was more powerful than me just telling her it wasn't a good idea. Don't miss what I said right there—have your advisor show you how giving money or paying off your home mortgage may affect your plan long-term. Seeing the effects with your own eyes is powerful.

As tears welled up in her eyes, I reiterated that she did the right thing, and that her daughter would benefit better in the long run by not having to become a caregiver if her mother ever had long-term health issues. Sometimes we need to hear it multiple times to know that we made the right decision. Ultimately, she took my advice and continued to stand strong and retain the money in her investment accounts. Way to go, Mama!

These are the typical stories that go on day after day in people's lives—grown children who haven't figured out how to take care of themselves and are still needing to rely on Mom or Dad—and usually the requests fall on Mom's servant heart. We need to know what we have in terms of money and then see clearly how our choices might play out. When we have a clear plan, it makes decisions like this much *simpler*—but not easy.

Stay strong, woman! You need to take care of you, and you deserve to feel secure.

WHAT GOT YOU THERE WON'T KEEP YOU THERE

I am a lifelong athlete.

I began as a competitive swimmer at the age of seven, burning out by the end of sixth grade with six practices a week. I was done with swimming, but I was just getting started on athletics and wanted to try all I could while I could. I dabbled in gymnastics but soon grew taller than the instructor. I excelled in basketball, softball, and track. But the sport that truly won my heart was volleyball. The teamwork, finesse, and aggressiveness drew me in—as did the coaches who mentored me. Spiking a ball at someone was often a terrifically satisfying experience, and I took a devious pleasure in seeing my opponent's wince.

Sports are a fantastic way for a woman to express herself. On a field, in a pool, or on the court, it's you and your instincts. There, we have space to move and feel our power. Athletics build our self-confidence and teach us to be better decision-makers. Of course, regular physical activity is extremely important, but it's more than coordination and sweat; we learn all sorts of life lessons while preparing, training, and playing. As women, sports offer deep opportunities to learn about ourselves.

The first time I played volleyball, I was hooked. My mom worked weekends to pay for me to play year-round. Through school, I also played the other sports—for fun, of course. Volleyball took me to be a Division I athlete at the University of Washington.

Obviously, I knew how to do the *sports thing*. But I felt a kind of new beginning, later in life, when I decided to do my first endurance race and hike 29,029 vertical feet in 36 hours.

I am built to be a sprinter. All the sports I played required short bursts of energy. In volleyball, we'd pass a ball back and forth over a net until it hit the ground. Then, we'd rest, reset, and do it again. In track, I'd run the 100- or 200-meter hurdles or compete in the long jump. The events required twenty seconds or less of explosive energy, then rest, resetting, and doing it one or two more times. In swimming, I rarely swam more than a 200-meter race. Usually, I competed in the 50- or 100-meter freestyle or butterfly. The events took less than sixty seconds, and then there were hours of rest until the next race.

When I accepted a business associate's challenge to participate in the *29029 Everesting* challenge, I wasn't prepared for how much different it would be from all my other training. Many of my friends were not at all surprised by my decision to do 29029, though the congratulatory acceptance email from the business associate did say I would "grow as a man." It appeared that he did not expect any women to sign up for the challenge (as I was the only woman who did accept out of the thirteen spots offered).

Those that knew me well quipped, "You're built for that stuff. It'll be easy for you!" How misinformed they were!

Training for an endurance hike is wildly different from sprinting and short-distance exercise. It required me to think entirely differently about how I ate, when I hiked, how often I trained, and what my recovery was. My lungs, legs and mind had quite an awakening! Initially, I was anxious in my preparation, and wasn't seeing the kind of performance I thought would get me through. But then I hired a coach who laid out a simple, easy-to-follow plan that was uniquely suited to endurance hiking.

Lesson learned: *when you are doing something strenuous and new, you'll want help from an expert who knows how to get things done!*

This translates perfectly to the kind of financial work I've done for decades (and now train other advisors across the nation to do): I've met thousands of individuals who have done a great job accumulating wealth. Maybe you did it yourself, or perhaps you hired an advisor who specializes in growing, saving, and accumulating wealth. Even though I had great coaches in years gone by, their direction about how to prepare myself for volleyball, softball, swimming, or short-distance races in track didn't help me in preparing to hike a mountain with altitude, 25 to 40 percent grade and exhausting heat. It didn't matter that Bill Gillespie, my weightlifting coach at UW, set the world record in beach press. He was not going to know how to equip my legs and body for what lie ahead, but my trainer, Brent Pease, who ran IRONMAN® triathlons, would.

Training as an individual for an IRONMAN® triathlon is a task most of us will never conceive to tackle, yet on October 13, 2018, Brent and his brother Kyle crossed the finish line at the IRONMAN® World Championships in Kona, HI, as the second ever adaptive team in history to complete it. Kyle has Cerebral Palsy, and they created the Kyle Pease Foundation—a nonprofit that helps disabled athletes participate and succeed in sports (I highly recommend searching for it on YouTube and reading their book). But I thought, if Brent could train himself to tow his brother in a kayak for a 2.4-mile swim, push an adaptive wheelchair for a 26.2-mile run, and then peddle him on a bike for 112 miles, this guy could train me to hike for 30+ hours straight up a mountain (and Brent was so good he was able to help my teenage son, Ashton, complete a 29029 with me just one week after his eighteenth birthday)!

We just need to hire the right coach for the race we have ahead.

Accumulating assets while in your twenties, thirties and early forties requires one set of skills. But when you approach your fifties and are nearing *de*cumulation, this stage of the journey requires a totally new set of skills and coaching. What got you there will not automatically keep you there.

Let me repeat: *what got you there might not keep you there.*

LIMITED PRODUCTS MEANS LIMITED OPTIONS

"Is there a way my twenty-two-year-old can get temporary car insurance on our less expensive vehicle?"

As our oldest son, Morgan, graduated and returned home to Seattle from college in Phoenix, he needed to be able to use one of our cars from time to time. His main ride, a motorcycle, wasn't going to be as exciting in the Seattle winter. Until he sold it and got his own car, we wanted to be sure we were appropriately covered.

We reached out to our Allstate agent. We learned we could put him on our policy, but that required Morgan to be covered on both our vehicles, which are much nicer than a new college grad would ideally drive. When they told us it would cost $224 per month to add him, I nearly fell out of my chair. What? Why? Allstate said that was the only way to do it, by fully adding him to our policy (and both vehicles). So, I decided to reach out to an insurance broker that had more than just Allstate products to offer.

I called the broker and asked her about options for our son. She said it was simple: we could get a "non-owner" insurance policy. That would give him coverage to drive any of our cars, or a friend's car. The cost was $79 per month. I asked the next logical question: "Why didn't Allstate offer me that?" Well, come to find out, they don't have access to that type of policy. It isn't in their menu of offerings.

Grrr. *That's not right.*

She described the very significant difference between working with a proprietary company like Allstate, which only offers Allstate products, versus a broker who can offer any line of insurance from a myriad of companies. The broker had the whole world of insurance options available to meet our specific needs, as opposed to Allstate, which provides fewer options and just gave me the products they carried.

I learned a valuable lesson that day as we obtained insurance for Morgan at $79 per month. We also found a new auto insurance provider.

That is the essence of working with an independent fiduciary.

HIRE A FIDUCIARY

A fiduciary is someone who is entrusted with the care of money or property and has a legal obligation to act in the best interest of another human being. They are not a salesperson, nor are they a babysitter. The role of the fiduciary is to look out for your very best interests and do things right, with integrity. Specifically, fiduciary duties include the responsibilities of care, confidentiality, loyalty, obedience, and accounting.

Being a fiduciary is very important component of who you choose to work with. They are held to a higher standard of charge for their clients; this should be a determining factor with any advisor you work with. You don't want to settle for an advisor that is limited to the products that are pushed by their parent company.

Allstate, Geico, or Progressive are the car insurance equivalent of many well-intentioned financial firms that offer only a certain range of products or investments. The advisors or agents who work for them are going to offer you the "best" of what they have, but what if some other company down the street has an even better product? The Allstate, Geico, or Progressive agent can't offer that to you, because they are tied to their brand's limited menu. Independent fiduciaries have a wider range of products and investments they can recommend and can offer more customized advice.

So, it is very simple. Ask your advisor, "Are you independent, and are you a fiduciary?" If the answer is "no," then I recommend you keep interviewing advisors.

After you begin meeting with an advisor, I also recommend you type their name into BrokerCheck. This is a free tool from FINRA (Financial Industry Regulatory Authority is a government-authorized not-for-profit organization) that can help you research the professional backgrounds of brokers and brokerage firms, as well as investment advisor firms and advisors. BrokerCheck is a trusted tool that shows you employment history, certifications, licenses, and any violations listed for brokers and investment advisors.

DON'T STOP AT ONE

Interview a few advisors during your search. Just like selecting a doctor, you want to make sure you can communicate easily, you can speak openly without fear of rejection, ridicule, or judgment, and that you feel good being around that individual. Stand up for yourself. Get what you need, ask questions, and be honest—don't settle. Talk to the advisor's team too. You can find out a lot about parents by speaking to their kids, and the same goes for team members who work for the advisor. Since solid planning takes a great team, you will often be working with support staff along your journey, just like a nurse or receptionist at a doctor's office. Make sure you like the whole package. Otherwise, keep looking.

Do your research, ask for references (yes, you can do that), and then trust your intuition. Women's intuition is often right, even if you can't explain it.

You may be introduced to a financial advisor by friends or family members, but please don't select someone simply because your brother works with them. You have the right to choose, and it's profoundly important that you get the individualized attention you need for the time of life you are in *right now*.

> *Back to basics: fundamentals and execution. They may not be sexy, but they'll help you win the race.*

MOST IMPORTANT TAKEAWAYS

1. There is a big difference between investing and retirement planning. Investing is the tools, planning is the process.

2. You need to be coachable to change. What got you there won't necessarily keep you there.

3. Don't let grown kids dictate your future security. You earned this time to be selfish. Taking proper care of yourself will help your children in the bigger picture of their life.

4. Hire an independent fiduciary.

5. Trust your gut, even if you can't explain it, and ask for references.

NEXT STEPS

1. Say out loud, "I am coachable and willing to change. I provide value for many people. I deserve a sound financial plan for my life!"

2. Get a written plan. Reach out this week to an advisor to build you a comprehensive view of what you currently own. And stay involved; even the greatest financial plan is of little use if you do not understand it. *YOU ARE HERE.*

3. Pick up your phone or shoot off a quick email asking your current advisor if they are a fiduciary. You have every right to probe. If they aren't, seriously consider a change and begin interviewing others.

CHAPTER 13

GETTING STARTED & ORGANIZED

> *Just take one step. That may be your greatest success today.*

I'M MARRIED—WHAT ABOUT MY SPOUSE?

If you are a married woman (or you and your partner have co-mingled finances), you might be thinking, "Well, my spouse isn't reading this. I don't know if they'll want to come in with me. I don't know if *I want them to come in with me.*" It's alright to have an initial visit with an advisor by yourself if you want or need to. Sometimes women have questions they would rather ask on their own without the frustrated rolling eyes of a partner or spouse. You may feel the need for a little space as you investigate new things in your life.

Yet remember that your marriage makes you a team, and financial planning requires the both of you, so they need to be involved after that first meeting if you go in alone.

It's wonderful to learn, and even more wonderful to learn *together*.

Fidelity Investments conducted a recent study that showed couples that work with a financial advisor are more likely to agree on a vision for retirement, find it easier have start money conversations, and feel more confident about their financial health[43]. And yet, only 57 percent of married respondents said they make retirement and investment planning decisions together. It's highly common for one partner to take the lead.

If you see yourself and your spouse in that statistic, please don't allow confusion or potential resistance to stop you from making forward progress. Your future well-being and peace of mind is more important than the discomfort of a confrontation. Many marriage fights are about money (I would know), but bringing in a "money therapist" (a.k.a. a financial advisor) can help you settle some of those unknowns that cause fear and anxiety between spouses, and help bridge the gap between how you both see things. Remember, there is no right or wrong, merely *different*.

A great advisor, male or female, will be able to provide direction, guidance, and, ultimately, hope.

As a fiduciary, it was deeply important for me to always leave an individual, be it a prospect, a client, a co-worker, or a friend, better than they were before we met. That was the mantra for our entire Becker Retirement team, and it was the central focus for everything we did.

As you now move forward in your life and financial journey, I want you to feel excited by the options at hand. Taking responsibility means that you will get the results you want, rather than just waiting to see what happens. You have the power to choose who will help

---

[43] FIDELITY INVESTMENTS® 2021 Couples & Money Study. https://www.fidelity.com/bin-public/060_www_fidelity_com/documents/about-fidelity/Fidelity-Couples-and-Money-Fact-Sheet-2021.pdf

you along this journey, which means you should accept nothing but the best.

There are great people to work with in your community, but remember—with today's remote working marketplace, you have access to incredible resources across the nation! You are not limited to time or geography, which makes it even more exciting to start having these conversations.

You may have received this book from one of the incredible advisors I personally mentor, but if not, reach out to my team at arwen@lifewitharwen.com and we can connect you virtually with an advisor that specializes in working with women and shares the same philosophy that I do. The pandemic showed advisors very clearly how successful we could be leading individuals and couples through these meaningful and important conversations through Zoom, and have a mutually beneficial (and effective) relationship.

WHERE TO GO FROM HERE

I am thrilled to share this book with you as a self-empowerment and educational guide. Now, you have an idea of what good planning looks like and, more importantly, what it feels like. Wherever you are in your life, however things currently are with your finances, now is just the right time to get started. Carve out some space to reflect on the topics that have most called to you in these pages, and please take advantage of the questions and action steps I've written at the end of each chapter. They are there to help you learn, meditate, and take yourself seriously (then follow up this with David Bach's bestseller, *Smart Women Finish Rich*, to continue laying the necessary foundation for financial success).

Make a list of the most pressing financial questions you have on your mind. If you already have a financial advisor, and you are happy with this individual, ask for a meeting or a call to go over those questions. If you are married, talk to your spouse about your questions, and, if it's comfortable, let them know what you are learning and doing research.

What do I really want?
What makes me truly happy?
What is most important to me?
What am I afraid of?
What do I need right now?

FIND YOUR MOUNTAIN AND BEGIN THE CLIMB

We have but one life.

You are reading this book because you feel ready for a better life. You're hungry for more, and you want to be your most glorious and authentic self. You want to be seen and heard! So, it's time to take steps forward.

I'm not proposing you do an obstacle course with a finish line, nor am I suggesting that you merely sit back and watch. Change is more than just a nice idea. Apply yourself, feel your desires, develop new habits, and make it personal. You won't get the freedom or the benefits if you don't do the work!

As previously mentioned, I committed to doing my first ever endurance race on my 47th birthday. As an adoring wife and mother of three young men, I decided to do this hike as a gift to myself—a reminder that I am strong, capable, and ready to push myself totally out of my comfort zone. I also wanted to do it to inspire other women to demand more of themselves, as well. You may recall I was emailed a congratulations note that I would "grow as a man" by accepting the hiking challenge, so I really wanted to show the doubters that women are competent and powerful. I wanted to set a giant goal and succeed, and do something very different.

Now, here's the twist in that story. I trained for months before the hike to prepare myself. I was fit and ready. But in the weeks before my Utah hike, 3,000 feet into my practice 13,000-foot hike that day, my hip flexor started to hurt. Every time I lifted my right leg to step up the mountain it felt like a massive cramp. Very uncomfortable to say the least, but especially when you recognize that, come race day, I would have another 25,000 vertical feet to still climb. There was no way I wanted to go into the big event with that kind of pain.

So, what to do? Recall my entry, cancel everything, and go home to rest it off for the next eight weeks? Feel sorry for myself, eat pints of ice cream, and fall into depression? Pretend nothing was wrong, and push harder, despite the agonizing pain?

OBSTACLES ARE A PART OF LIFE'S JOURNEY

I took the rational road and never lost sight of my goal. I spoke to a physical therapist, to my sports chiropractor, and to my coach, who all told me that the way to relieve the hip pain was to balance the weak muscles around it (namely my glutes) and to do heat-therapy (not ice-therapy as I was doing). I needed to work on the entire area's mobility and balance my muscle strength. The therapist and coach gave me a list of exercises to do daily, while my chiropractor kept things aligned and together as we reinforced the right muscles.

I was the one in pain, so I had to do the recovery work. Each day, I made a choice to follow through on those prescribed exercises (most of which made me feel quite weak and out of shape). I could just as easily make some excuses or say I was too busy, and let a few days slide. But then, I'd have had no improvement. The specialist understood my problem and gave me a diagnosis, along with a solution. Yet it was up to me to take care of myself. No one else would be feeling the pain, so it was up to me to take care of myself. I had to want the relief before I could do something about it.

I did those exercises, and when I went to Utah to do my giant hike in August, I didn't suffer a single moment of pain. Those daily decisions to do the small, and seemingly insignificant, work made all the difference. I hiked the Everest equivalent, making 112,818 steps in 32 hours. Vertical feet means upwards—towards the sky. There was no horizontal walking. And I didn't have a single moment of hurt.

SEEK HELP FROM EXPERTS

I was suffering, but I sought help from experts I could trust. We made a healing plan and I followed that path daily with tiny bouts of courage and commitment. I reached my goal pain-free and went farther than I ever thought I could. As it is said, you don't know what your abilities are until you make a full commitment to developing them.

Are you willing to put in the work? Do you see the benefits ahead, and are you excited by all the amazing ways your life can and will change? Does freedom and financial peace sound good to you?

Now, I realize that some of you reading this may not be totally ready to take things on full-speed. You may feel curious but are not yet convinced that you want to take your finances seriously. Maybe it feels too heavy, or you are just afraid. Maybe there are relationship issues you need to work on first. I understand. Each of us is unique, and I am not at all one to judge.

Now, I'm not asking you to hike up a mountain. I'm not saying you need to become a financial guru, or join a special membership club. I'm simply sending you an invitation to your own life!

It took me a long time to have my own awakening. The process spanned between my mid-twenties divorce until the Great Recession, when I finally began taking things seriously. It was basically fifteen years of knowing I needed to change something, without really knowing how. I am certainly not an overnight success.

Even after I did start to educate myself, it took me ten more years to feel truly financially secure in what I knew, how it was being managed, and ultimately how it would keep me safe for the future. Great accomplishments take time. Just like a massive hike, it is all about focusing on one step at a time. Don't look up at the daunting mountain peak—just keep your eyes on where your foot goes, next.

> *"Most people overestimate what they can do in one year and underestimate what they can do in ten years."* – BILL GATES

DON'T WAIT TO FEEL READY

Until you have clarity about your own situation and the pain you may (or may not) feel—please know that you don't need to *feel* ready to make that initial appointment. Feeling ready is a lie. Waiting for the time when you *feel ready* is a way to keep you stuck in your circumstance and mediocrity, and not achieve your God-given destiny. It doesn't require any financial confidence to talk to someone with financial knowledge. It requires courage. And a great advisor knows that they are there to be your educator and helper, not to shame you for what you don't know. And reading this book is honestly the best possible start to your new, confident financial life! Without knowing it, you've already gotten yourself on the high road.

Believe it when I tell you, you are not alone in the way you feel. Most women I have spoken with do not feel ready. That is why you hire an advisor. Knowing more about yourself and your own financial history (events, family, emotions) gives you a starting place. You can talk about this book and your reactions while reading. You can bring up certain sections and terms. Show where you've made highlights. Circle things, and write notes to yourself. If there is a particular section that really resonates with you, draw a giant star next to it, and ask yourself *why*. Show it to your sister, show it to your best friend, and ask what they think. That will get the conversation going.

And, even if you aren't ready to face your own situation—please do consider the well-being of your children and family. They need you to take it seriously. They need you to be in the best shape possible, and they worry about you. Furthermore, you need to set a good example for those you love, and set a pace of safety and responsibility for the entire family. If you aren't ready to act out of conviction, enthusiasm, or even pain, do it out of love!

Start by talking with your partner, spouse, or a close confidant. Let them know that you are taking strides and learning, and open an ongoing conversation. Talking about money is key to nurturing a closer connection with your partner and yourself. Don't be afraid at all to talk about finances with your girlfriends, either, because it can be a great opportunity for accountability while also helping to educate each other. Women like to talk about all sorts of things, but we often hesitate to mention money because it feels intimidating or even taboo. Break the ice, and let the conversations flow. We need to normalize the idea that it's healthy to talk about money, and doing so can be empowering. Not only will you feel more bonded, but it will allow you to freely talk about your progress, emotions, goals, and triumphs, and move forward together. Share this book when you feel comfortable, and speak to your daughters and granddaughters, too.

SELF-LIMITING BELIEFS NEED TO GO

Have you fallen into the trap of thinking a "man will be your plan?" What kind of role model are you presenting to the younger women in your family and community? What female stereotypes are you hiding behind? Are you afraid you are too old to learn anything new? Do you think it is too soon to start planning for retirement and will put it off for another day? You don't want to rock the boat? Afraid to use your voice? Think it's all just too complicated? Think again!

Men in our culture are encouraged to be financial brains and leaders, and they use networking to share their insights and ideas. Women should be doing the same, without any sort of guilt or shame. How is it that we can comfortably discuss the most intimate details of our pregnancies, trials in our marriages, issues in the workplace, and drama from relationships, but we hold back on ever mentioning the word *investment?*

Fidelity Investments did a fascinating study on women and money[44], and found that 83 percent of women questioned were keen to learn more about their finances, while eight in ten women said they avoided conversations about their finances with their closest friends and family. The reasons being that it felt too personal, they didn't want to sound dumb, or they were raised in a family that taught them not to approach the topic at all. Moreover, 77 percent of women respondents felt confident discussing medical issues with a doctor on their own, while only 47 percent would be comfortable talking about money and investing with a financial professional. But this fear towards talking about money with our friends, family, and partners extends far further, and prevents us from taking responsibility for our financial well-being.

Once and for all, let's change the narrative around women and money, and set ourselves strong and free. We can do this, and we can handle it—one step and one conversation at a time.

"Dig deep—get deliberate, inspired, and going." – BRENÉ BROWN

Be willing to question your current situation. Your future self will thank you for it. Get out there, sister, and handle it!

> *Consistency and commitment are constant traits in a successful and meaningful life.*

---

44 Fidelity Investments, MONEY FIT WOMEN STUDY: Executive Summary (2015). https://www.fidelity.com/bin-public/060_www_fidelity_com/documents/women-fit-money-study.pdf

MOST IMPORTANT TAKEAWAYS

1. Meeting with a retirement planner is designed to provide hope and clarity related to your current direction.

2. An advisor can work with you in person or over the phone/computer. You are not limited to meeting in an office somewhere in the city. If you are struggling to find a great advisor in your area, contact my team at *arwen@lifewitharwen.com* and we can connect you virtually with one of the many advisors I have mentored and who specialize in this type of work with women.

3. If your financial advisor isn't one that specializes in retirement planning, it may be time to look around for one who is an independent fiduciary that does.

4. It is okay to question your spouse and take the lead at getting outside help from a professional. Even if your spouse isn't *on board* when you start the process, you may be pleasantly surprised to see them come around after holding a clear plan in their hands.

NEXT STEP:

1. Start today! Schedule a time with a few planners to see if they have the capability to do all the things we have talked about. There are thousands of tremendous, caring advisors who can do all that I have mentioned. Keep looking until you find one and you like how they communicate. This relationship may last ten, twenty, or more years, so be diligent and get what you want and need (again, reach out to my team if you need some referrals to an advisor you could work with virtually).

2. Read multiple financial books and ask for recommendations from friends or associates you admire financially, but you can certainly

begin with those books I listed in the resources at the back, as well as the financial podcasts I highlighted for women.

3. Tell a friend or someone you trust in your inner circle that you are reading this book and making some life changes. Open up the conversation and see where it takes you—you may be pleasantly surprised! You'll plant seeds of trust for the future, shining light on a vital topic that we generally don't talk about.

CHAPTER 14

CONCLUSION

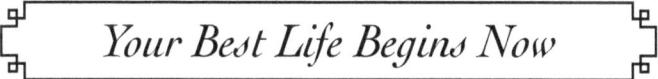
Your Best Life Begins Now

REFUSE TO LIVE A LIFE OF REGRET

Change is difficult. Distractions are real. Life is pulling at you from all directions. I know what it's like to want to give up when things feel out of control. I know what it's like to feel buried by debt and turmoil. One choice in late 2016 changed my life forever and led me to *you*.

I had hit my breaking point, and I was plenty ready to throw in the towel. After landing myself in the ER thinking I was having a heart attack (nope, it was just debilitating stress), I took to drastic measures and decided that I needed to sell our seventeen-year financial planning company because things were hard and not working. The financial strain from digging out from the Great Recession had my body fatigued and my mind exhausted. I ached for relief from the struggle, it was time to waive the white flag of surrender and quit. I deserved to be happy (or so my mind kept telling me).

We found a buyer, but at the last minute, I called off the sale believing it would be the end to our marriage. I recognized that my husband, company, employees, and clients meant more to me, but something major had to change. Then I realized, *it's okay to want to quit, just don't*. I was being called forth to shift the direction of our company. That fateful day of September 25, 2016 was the turning point that led me to take over all the marketing of our company and shift our collective focus onto something new.

My husband had done incredible work for the prior seventeen years, being the face and voice of our firm. Just like me, he was tired of the same ol' thing. He was happy to pass that role and support me in the same way I had supported him for all those years. I realized that I was being called to turn the focus of our company on to the underserved members of our community: *women*.

Women. Mothers. Daughters. Sisters. Aunts. Nieces. The last woman standing. *You*.

During that time of darkness, a light appeared, leading me forward. In the next eight years, I became an expert in marketing financial services to women. As with most cases, it wasn't an instant success. It happened as we did the work, one step at a time, and that work compounded over the years.

There was such a deep need in my area—a never-ending well of women needing direction—but what about the women in all the other cities of our nation? Who was going to inspire them, listen to them, help them, and light them up to believe in their own greatness? Who was going to alter how the financial services industry approaches and deals with women? Along with my motivation to serve the women in our region, another passion has moved me into what I'm doing now: training some of most thoughtful and capable advisors around the country to better serve the women in their communities. They are helping to change the world *one woman at a time*. Thus, my LIFE with Arwen training organization was born.

After so many years leading Becker Retirement Group forward with a focus on women and their financial well-being, it gave me all the tools needed to train both men and women advisors across the country to do the same. What a blessing—to be able to educate and energize on both sides of the need! I was helping women clients understand from the ground up, and teaching advisors how to appreciate and serve those female clients better.

This gave me a newfound intention for the next phase of my life and career. Following the belief in my God-given purpose, changing lives became paramount and our financial benefit became secondary. The desire for impact drove me; I needed to do what was right for the women who were so overlooked and left out of money discussions.

I grew as a person—as a woman, as a wife, as a mother, a friend, a speaker, and as a business owner. Moreover, we were blessed with tremendous financial security as we worked further into the integrity of our purpose. Service became the most important driver of our company and influence. I handled it, my part. I finally quit making everyone else responsible for what I needed to do. For the first time in my life, I feel authentic, radiant, powerful, and secure in who I am—it's awesome!

NOW IT'S YOUR TURN

You know what you need to do; now you just need to start. No one is going to do this for you. There is no knight in shining armor to save you from all your hurt and struggle. No one is your financial plan. The pot o' gold isn't waiting at the end of the proverbial rainbow. You are tired of gasping for air. Your excuses and fear are an illusion that will only keep you stuck. You aren't drinking this Kool-Aid. Now, your eyes are open.

I'm gonna handle this! Say it out loud. *I'm gonna handle this! I've got this! I am worthy and able! I am a highly capable woman! I am learning more everyday! I matter to many people! I will handle this! My time is now! No more indecision! I am doing this!*

The planning you do today isn't just about you—it's about the generations to come.

Your legacy starts today.

Pick up the phone. Make the call. Do the research. Take financial inventory. Interview some advisors. Talk to people you look up to in the area of personal finances. Get direction and start moving. God can only direct you when you are moving, not when you are standing still. Move; even if it ends up being the wrong direction, you will get set on the right path!

Think of a great woman you admire in history. Did she allow others or life to push her around? Did she let her fear hold her back from her dreams and what she believed in for her life? Did she put her happiness in the hands of other people? You know the answer: *no,* she handled it!

This is just the beginning of something amazing and miraculous. You are a part of something bigger than yourself. You are part of a movement. A movement of women, women who are not willing to sit back and let someone else dictate their lives. Who don't believe the lies saying they are flaky or indecisive. Women who refuse to agree that understanding personal finance is a *man's job* because the financial industry struggles to pivot and speak to the real players—you.

You ready for this new game? *I've got your back.*

Look at you, transitioning into your destiny. Not a little wallflower, but a bad-ass chick! I'm so proud of you. You did what I knew you would.

The pages are turning and the dark clouds are washing away.

Congratulations, my dear...

You handled it!

RESOURCES:
BECOMING A BETTER HUMAN

RECOMMENDED FINANCIAL BOOKS:

Smart Women Finish Rich by David Bach

Women with Money by Jean Chatzky

The Simple Path to Wealth by J.L. Collins

Worth It by Amanda Steinberg

On My Own Two Feet by Manisha Thakor and Sharon Kedar

You are a Badass at Making Money by Jen Sincero

I Will Teach You to be Rich by Ramit Sethi

Your Money or Your Life by Vicki Robin and Joe Dominguez

Wealth for Women by Bonnie Koo

The Index Card by Helaine Olen and Harold Pollack

RECOMMENDED FINANCIAL PODCASTS:

Clever Girls Know with Bola Sokunbi

So Money with Farnoosh Torabi

Money Confidential with Stefanie O'Connell Rodriquez

Money With Katie with Katie Gattie Tassin

Afford Anything with Paula Pant

RECOMMENDED MOTIVATIONAL BOOKS (THAT TRULY CHANGED ARWEN'S LIFE):

Being Happy! by Andrew Matthews

How to Win Friends and Influence People by Dale Carnegie

The 5 Love Languages by Gary Chapman

How to Have Confidence and Power in Dealing with People by Les Giblin

Battlefield of the Mind by Joyce Meyer

Saving Your (Second) Marriage Before It Starts by Drs. Les and Leslie Parrott

Ego is the Enemy by Ryan Holiday

Obstacle is the Way by Ryan Holiday

Stillness is the Key by Ryan Holiday

Roar (How to Match your Food and Fitness to Your Female Physiology for Optimum Performance, Great Health, and a Strong, Lean Body for Life) by Stacy Sims, PhD

Next Level (Your Guide to Kicking Ass, Feeling Great, and Crushing Goals Through Menopause and Beyond) by Stacy Sims, PhD

Alcohol Lied to Me by Craig Beck

You'll Get Through This by Max Lucado

The Assertiveness Guide for Women by Julie De Azevedo Hanks, PhD

Adult Children of Alcoholics by Janet Geringer Woititz, Ed.D.

Love Like You've Never Been Hurt by Jentezen Franklin

The Enemies of Excellence by Greg Salciccioli

Think Better Live Better by Joel Osteen

RECOMMENDED INSPIRATIONAL PODCASTS:

She Handled It!® with Arwen Becker

Goal Digger with Jenna Kutcher

Sober Powered with Gill

Real Talk Kim with Kim Jones

True Grit and Grace with Amberly Lago

Women of Impact with Lisa Bilyeu

Achieve Your Goals with Hal Elrod

The Ed Mylett Show with Ed Mylett

Compared to Who? (Biblical Approach to Body Image) by Heather Creekmore

Faith Over Fear by Jennifer Slattery

Crazy Little Thing Called Marriage with Greg and Erin Smalley

School of Greatness with Lewis Howes

RECOMMENDED YOUVERSION (BIBLE.COM) DEVOTIONALS:

Women and Money – She Handled It!®

Retirement: Insights from the Bible

Thrive in Retirement

Restful Anticipation: Finding Contentment in Seasons of Waiting

7 Days of New Beginnings

Level Up: Big Growth Through Small Actions

Navigating Life's Transitions

Legacy Leadership

ABOUT THE AUTHOR

Arwen Becker has helped thousands of women live a better financial life. She spent many years as a financial advisor and twenty-two years as co-owner of Becker Retirement Group with her husband Randy. In June of 2022, they sold their retirement planning firm, affording her the opportunity to focus full-time on her purpose: inspiring and empowering women to rise up and take financial responsibility. Her passion is training financial advisors and planners across the nation to serve women more effectively, thus improving how the financial industry speaks to and educates women.

She is a national keynote speaker, author and contributor to multiple books, the host of the *She Handled It!*® podcast, creator of the YouVersion *Women & Money* devotional, and is often featured as a guest expert on TD Ameritrade Network, Yahoo Finance, and many other national news programs.

Arwen and Randy are proud parents of Morgan, Ashton, and Easton. She takes pleasure in traveling, crafting, serving her local church, and enjoys exploring low tide near her family's beach house on the Puget Sound. Arwen is an endurance athlete, who enjoys early morning runs and long day hikes in the Pacific Northwest with her family and friends.

SPECIAL THANKS

There are many individuals that have helped me along this journey and had an impact on me, whether minor or major. There are more people than I could possibly thank, but I will sure try!

Above all, I must thank God for putting this passion in me in May 2017, a spark that has been fanned by many along the way and tried to be extinguished by others… What God has created; no man can eliminate. Thank you, Lord, that it's now burning bright!

To the most important relationship I have here on earth, my incredibly loving, supportive, and amazing husband, Randy: you have stood alongside me as I have worked my way through this calling that's been placed in my life, even through the times that impeded my focus at Becker Retirement Group. You raised up and took greater responsibility at BRG while I was sorting through this drive that was still somewhat directionless. You continued to love me along the way, financially supported this passion, and stood in faith that eventually it would pay us back in spades. You allowed me to transition our company to focus on heavily on women, an area that was underserved and misunderstood. You then showed the industry that a company of mostly male advisors could thrive in supporting women in this way…it wasn't just a woman thing. Thank God you didn't give up on me and my crazy dream! I love you more than I could ever say and continue to look forward to many wonderful experiences with you!

To our three boys, Morgan, Ashton, and Easton, for encouraging me to head to the cabin to write my books, helping serve many of our clients over the years at dozens of events, and for humoring me as I asked you to dress up in costumes for the annual client birthday card…you guys may have complained a little bit, but in the end you were great sports! I am also so blessed to now have a beautiful, kind daughter-in-law, Morgan (yes, she is married to our son with the same first name)…seeing the joy and completeness you bring to our son is all I could ever ask for. Our entire family's world is better because you are now in it and I thank you for always giving me a kind word, encouraging call and being so gracious! I love you "kids" with all my heart!

To my mom, Donna, thank you for never giving up and truly walking out what it means to be faithful in the little things. You have always proved that it isn't how you start the race, it is how you finish. You are kind, consistent and a truly wonderful human being. I am grateful that God gave me you as my mom and I hope that your legacy and impact on me encourages many other women to believe in what is possible. Thanks for letting me tell your story!

To my sister, Mindi, who brings a smile to the faces of people you meet along the way, and for being one of my inspirations to finally give up alcohol for good…very few choices I've made have been so impactful. Thanks for being willing to walk it out in your own life first and inspire me to do so in my own!

To my wonderful Grandma Hazel…you may not be here on earth, but I know you are peering down on me from heaven, standing in the presence of Jesus. You showed by example that a woman can live the life of her dreams even after being widowed twice, and that our latter years can be vibrant, full of color (red of course!) and extremely active. Proving that women can do anything; you can start modeling (and get your GED) in your fifties, date a long-haul trucker (with a potty mouth) in your seventies, wear high heels as you neared your eighties and never lose your elegance or faith in God even as you battled through cancer. Thank you also for being a classy woman that demonstrated what a life of following Christ looked like, not by force but by mercy and grace. Gosh do I miss you.

To some of the most supportive women in my entire life, my best friends Fahren Johnson and Junko Varsovia, for walking alongside me throughout the many changes of my life over the past fifteen years. The two of you are truly so special to me, and your lives and passion for those less fortunate continue to inspire me to do just a little bit more than I did yesterday...I love you both so much!

To Rakel Chafir, a woman on a mission to truly alter the world's view of a "mid-life woman." You helped me fully step into who I've been created to be, not apologize for it, and created space that was safe for me to expand and grow my life. Grazie Amore Mio!

To all the Becker Retirement Group women who have supported me along this journey and who fanned the flames of this belief I had that women deserved greater attention from financial advisors and my industry. To Shawna Burkholder, for all your wisdom, deep care for our clients, and helping to create a culture of service (and often saving Randy and me from marital arguments that would come home with us...ha-ha!). To Mackenzie Parfitt, for passion and belief in the mission of serving women, and a great ability to protect the sacred space we were creating in those rooms. To Karen Linscott, for taking a big role of responsibility off my shoulders and allowing me to turn my focus towards women and away from the in-depth running of much of the company. To Julie Steppan, for trusting us during the crazy pandemic to make a switch to our firm, for serving women wholeheartedly and becoming the teacher you always knew you could be, and most importantly for continuing Randy's thirty-six-year legacy. And to Sara Willy, for your encouragement, amazing smile, and incredible gift-giving and crafting skills. Without all of you over the last eight years, I would have let many of the naysayers alter my belief in what I knew to be true...thank you!

To David Bach, for your trust and belief in me for all those years that I was teaching *Smart Women, Smart Retirement*™ over and over. You have reached out via phone, text or email many times just when I needed it. Your friendship has mattered deeply to me, and I don't take it for granted. Many conversations that happened over these last eight years have benefited both Randy and me personally, professionally, and financially...thank you!

To all the incredible individuals we met through our partnership with Advisors Excel over the past eleven years, that helped us become a truly efficient and effective company, that had a fantastic culture of people and a true heart of service. Most notably, but certainly not limited to: Cody Foster, David Callanan, Bill Kentling (helping me find my voice and providing me encouragement in moments of doubt), Megan Mosack, Spencer Grosvenor, Cory Swain, LeAnne Rodriguez (one of the most joy-filled, encouraging women I know), Brian Theis, Matt Ewald, Jim Bowman, Phil Blosser, Sherri Pike, Jammie Serrano, Tana Akers (helping me fine-tune my message and express it powerfully through video), Kevin Johnson, and Alexis Burchett. To the hundreds of other people that we've interacted with over the years through creative design, radio, TV, wealth management, and all the back office support we could possibly need in our entire lives... thank you!

To Erica Pauly, thank you for helping me understand that I wasn't crazy, that marketing to women was, in fact, valuable and financially beneficial. You and your team help me put the data behind what I believed in my heart—thank you so much!

To Alex Hug and Mitch Schwab at Acquire Direct for truly leaning in and believing, as much as I did, that marketing to women was dramatically needed and vastly underserved. Thank you for putting your faith in me early on and showing me what we can do on a national scale when we work together!

To my one-woman PR team, Pam Reimer, for working so darn hard to book me some of the best national TV and radio interviews, which I've been able to repurpose over and over. You believed in my mission and were able to communicate it, and I appreciate all the work you've done!

To Shawn Sparks for giving me the best advice early on in my new journey, to not allow my passion project to be someone else's side hustle. That helped me to team up with those that were just as passionate and driven about serving women well as I was. Appreciate all you have done for both Randy and me over the last decade. Your friendship and coaching made us great!

To all the incredible mentees I've met through my training partnership with Next Level Advisors, individuals from across the country who have trusted me to impart all that I've learned over the years into your practice so you can better serve women in your communities… thank you so much for your trust in me! And, most importantly, to Brandon Stuerke for seeing something in me, following the prompting he felt from God, and helping me bring forth my training on a national scale in a scalable way that wasn't going to lose a part of me in the process. But, above all, for imparting my passion into hungry advisors who believe women deserve something different and better…thank you!

Special shout out to all the men who have the courage to go out there and teach *She Handled It!*® *Retirement* to women in their community; you are the warriors, boots on the ground, we can't impact women in a massive way without you!

A special thanks to Debbie Page and Alayne Reesberg, you both came into my life at the time in which my vision was small, my passion was big, and I needed some direction. Both of you provided wisdom and scaffolding for me when the wrong person could've easily torn it apart. Thanks for believing in me and providing me the tools I needed at the time. Both of you are always near and dear to my heart!

To all the wonderful humans at the start of this book that took the time to read my manuscript and write a testimonial…Amberly, Cathy, Judy, Mickey, Daphne, Stephanie, Wendy, Kerstin, Amber, Abby, Marcella, Megan, Eva, Sarah, Sheryl, your words mean a great deal to me, and I can't say thank you enough for your time and effort! Each of you believe women deserve more and are helping bring that change in your own world and vocations. THANK YOU!!!!!! An extra thanks to Mickey as I sincerely appreciated your additional effort and time to do a final read-through of my manuscript…you are such an encouragement to me!

To my social media maven, Taylor Renyer, thank you for taking all my content, repurposing it, and amplifying my voice in a world that is easily distracted. You've been a great support in furthering this mission and helping me enjoy content creation along the way!

To my wonderful assistant Rachel Elbe, thank you for walking along this new path with me and for your easy-going attitude, wonderful effort and for being a thinker! You are a woman who knows how to get things done. This journey is much more chill because you are helping me along the way!

To Chapman Fina, thank you for continuing to be a great example of a woman-owned business that truly cares for her community and the women she serves. You have been vital at clothing me with goodness, and being that fashion coach I needed to always look my best whether on stage, in the office or meeting amazing other women around the world. We need more businesses like Via Lago, that truly care for people, not just the bottom line! Appreciate you!

To Jeanette Bajalia for being the initial spark that helped me see a massive need I had no idea existed. You helped impart the long-term vision that women deserve something better, and that I could help further that mission.

To the best coach I could have ever had, Bill Gillespie, thank you! Your kind demeanor (with high expectations) was exactly what I needed in those challenging years at UW. As a driven teenager, you found a way to encourage the best within me while protecting the vulnerable broken parts I had, and I am forever grateful that you came to my defense when others were tearing me down. Not until decades later would I realize that your overwhelming grace came straight from your relationship with Christ which has molded you into one of the best human beings I have ever met. Thanks for showing by example that no matter our background, financial status, or home life, that hard work, dedication, and an unwillingness to quit, are traits we all can nurture and possess. Congrats on your world record 50 years in the making!!

To my incredible team at Vida Integrated Health, thank you for partnering with me in keeping my health in an optimal space so I can live fully into my purpose, reach more women, and live a very long, healthy life! Without all of you, but more notably Taunie, Kasey, Michaela, Chase, Ellie, and Jacque, I would be a lesser version of myself (and to Ben for helping Ashton complete 29029 with me after breaking his leg…you and Kasey were vital to his success and belief)…thank you!

To my 29029 Everesting family, you created a space for me to truly explore my physical capabilities in a massive, yet deeply moving way and I am a better person for it. Thank you for all that have poured into me and given me the opportunity to pour into others… you are not getting rid of me anytime soon; besides, the world needs more bubbles! I also am constantly meeting new incredible human beings through this community and never cease to be amazed at the will, grit, and determination of individuals from all walks of life. A special shout out to my coaches Brent and Ashley and the Voice of the Mountain, Colleen…adore you three and all you have done to enlarge my life!

To Churchome and Pastors Judah and Chelsea Smith, and Mark and Crystal Venti, for sowing into our family's lives since 2011. You, Chelsea, gave me an opportunity early on in my mission to speak to the church family about the importance of financial planning for women…that seed of belief you planted meant a great deal, and Crystal, you kept the enthusiastic encouragement flowing, thank you!

To my editor, Mindy King-Politini, you took the daunting task of updating, revising, and renewing this book and made it pretty darn simple. You understood what I was trying to communicate and helped me peer a little bit deeper into my audience's mind to truly get to the heart of the matter. You are a gifted communicator and the biggest cheerleader I had in the last year-long journey to write this book!

Finally, thanks to the thousands of women who have trusted me with their stories, and their pain and frustration with the financial industry...I hear you, and I am doing what I can in my power, and God's grace, to bring the change that the next generation needs. We're doing this, we're changing the world one woman at a time!

www.ingramcontent.com/pod-product-compliance
Lightning Source LLC
Chambersburg PA
CBHW061149170426
43209CB00035B/1952/J